A CHANGED PERSPECTIVE

An Essential Guide for Emerging Leaders

BOB EMILIANI

A Changed Perspective: An Essential Guide for Emerging Leaders / Bob Emiliani

Cover design by Bob Emiliani. The image of tree rings represents the growth of leaders' Knowledge-Reality Universe from KRU-I to KRU-II. Back cover photograph by Josh Edenbaum Photography.

ISBN-13: 978-1-7320191-6-4
Library of Congress Control Number: 2022922578

1. Leadership 2. Management 3. Business 4. Sociology
5. Preconceptions

First Edition: January 2023

Published by Cubic LLC, South Kingstown, Rhode Island, USA.

This publication is believed to provide accurate information with respect to the subject matter covered. It is sold with the understanding that it does not in any way represent legal, financial, business, consulting, or other professional service.

Manufactured using digital print-on-demand technology.

CONTENTS

Preface   vii

Introduction   1

1. Preconceptions   17

2. Dead Hand of the Past   41

3. Difficult Situations   63

4. Changing Your Perspective   93

Closing Comments   105

About the Author   115

♥ L

🙏 V

"History is strewn with the wreckage left by well-motivated individuals and groups, shattered by forces they did not comprehend and could not control."

- Douglas F. Dowd

Preface

In my most recent book, *The Aesthetic Compass: Foundation of Leadership Action and Inaction* (2022), I said:

> "This book represents the endpoint of a line of work that I began more than 15 years ago. Simply put, it is to understand why, as Jean-Baptiste Karr said more than 150 years ago, 'The more things change, the more they stay the same' [1]."

Turns out it was not the endpoint. It was unwise to make such a statement given my track record and that some ideas were still rumbling around in my head at the time *The Aesthetic Compass* was published. As is always the case, there remain questions unanswered that seize my curiosity and excitedly compel investigation and explication. Perhaps the present work will be the endpoint, perhaps not.

My efforts to understand the phenomenon expressed by Karr's words are in relation to the practical work of leading and managing organizations [2]. Despite a century of effort by untold numbers of people to deconstruct leadership – to understand it and identify better ways to lead and manage people – it has had little effect to narrow the range of acceptable leadership methods in organizations. Today, as with long ago, we see heavy-handed approaches to leadership and management in hierarchical organizations that suggest little has been learned since the time of ancient Egyptian Pharaohs [3]. Rights and privileges stand above all, destined to be preserved, whether in the 4th millennium BC or in

2023. How is it that so little can be learned over such a long stretch of time? Why is there so little transmittal of leadership thinking and practice of the type that engages and energizes people compared to that which neglects and discourages people? To state it simplistically, why is "command-and-control" still so popular among leaders, whether in good times or bad?

It seems that at any time and in any context, there is substantial dissatisfaction with leaders, resulting in lower employee engagement and productivity [4]. Is that simply the nature of leadership, unwilling to acknowledge the majority of followers needs? They want better leadership (Figure P-1), but most leaders are not interested in leading better. Perhaps they don't know what to do or don't care, despite access to resources and being in positions to deliver better leadership.

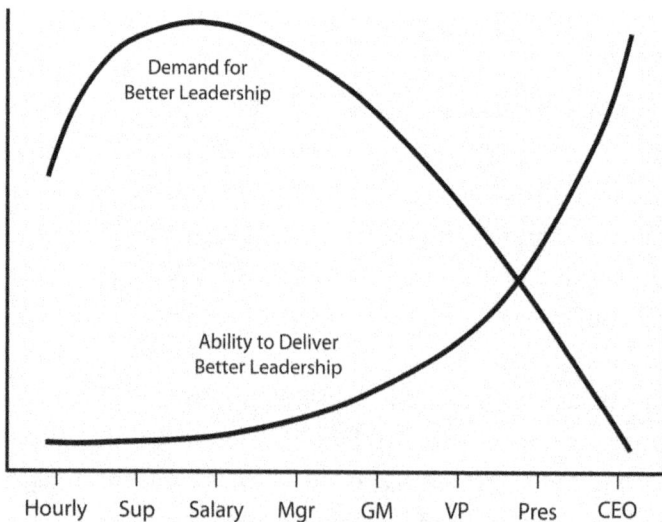

Figure P-1. Relationship between demand for better leaders and those in the positions to deliver it.

The durability of ancient ways of leading and managing people is an impediment to the human, organizational, and technological progress that must be made now and, in the future, to assure survival of the species. Unless, of course, the shared mindset of those in top leadership positions, at any given point in time, is that such progress is not a necessity. If so, it would be evidence of a preconception that human existence can only and forever be one where there are winners and losers. We can accept that preconception, or we can ask: "Why?" I always choose to ask "Why?" because it is both an intellectual and a practical challenge, one that can generate pathways for improvement and progress. The durability of ancient ways is worth understanding in the hope – perhaps remote hope – that it will someday improve how most organizations are led and managed.

I wanted to write this book to explore three important things. First, the role of preconceptions in guiding leaders' thinking and actions. Second, how difficult situations arise and why difficult situations are accepted by leaders as a *fait accompli*. Third, how can difficult situations be made less common and less difficult to reduce human stress and frustration and enable greater human flourishing on a resource constrained planet. To do that requires understanding how and why one generation of leaders after the another prefers stasis – inaction, delayed action, or very limited action – over more quickly and comprehensively responding to the dynamic, evolutionary existence that is fundamental to life, living, and the fulfillment of human needs.

The purpose of this book is to challenge the settled view that better leadership is brought about simply by changing leaders' behaviors [5]. While that may be true under certain circumstances, it imparts an illusion that it is true under all circumstances. However, in the socio-economic hierarchy of business and, more generally, organizations, behavior change at the top directed towards improved leadership and management is difficult and rare due to its high social and political costs. When it does occur, it is often short-lived. There is a regression to the norm of one's peers, whether they are living or long dead, to traditional ways of thinking and doing things. This suggests something much deeper is at work to not only thwart changes in behavior, but to assure continuity in behaviors over time for those who are in positions of leadership [6].

While peer pressure to conform to a set of behaviors is ever-present, this book is concerned with what lies below the surface. Rather than undertaking an analysis based on complicated social psychology or brain science, a simpler method will be used to illuminate the mindset that produces the observed leadership behaviors. We will examine what is in plain sight, either through leaders' words or though close observation of leaders' actions – to reveal what lies below.

To that end, the focus will be leaders' preconceptions and how preconceptions function to preserve the social status quo. We will also touch upon how leaders' preconceptions limit (i.e., thwart or delay) technological advancement when it is beneficial to them or others to do so. A common example is when leaders extinguish an innovation in favor of continuing an existing high margin product or service – e.g.,

Eastman Kodak leaders' decision not to pursue digital imaging in favor of the continued sale of photographic film and related products and services [7].

While established leaders may be interested in this book and benefit greatly from it, emerging leaders will be its greatest beneficiaries. Most established leaders are unlikely to have interest in challenging their preconceptions and changing how they think and act. Emerging leaders are more likely to do so, but they will unavoidably fall under the strong influence of more experienced leaders who will discourage changes in preconceptions. Further, most experienced leaders will not be receptive to pressure from emerging leaders to change their preconceptions. That will be a point of great conflict as they will insist you are the one in error.

Ultimately, this book seeks to answer the question – "What do I have to do to become a better leader?" – at its root. Understanding how preconceptions function to preserve the status quo [8] also opens the door to understating how preconceptions can overcome internal barriers to change when change is needed; to recognize the need for change and produce the required scope of change in a timely manner. My hope is that seeing things through the lens of preconceptions will produce a change in perspective among readers. For it is a changed perspective, far more than a change in behaviors, that generate the types of change that the times call for.

Bob Emiliani
Wakefield, Rhode Island
January 2023

Notes

[1] This epigram is attributed to Jean-Baptiste Alphonse Karr circa 1848: *"Plus ça change, plus c'est la même chose."* https://en.wikipedia.org/wiki/Jean-Baptiste_Alphonse _Karr, accessed 20 November 2022

[2] See the four-book series: Emiliani, B. (2018), *The Triumph of Classical Management Over Lean Management: How Tradition Prevails and What to Do About It*, Cubic LLC, South Kingstown, Rhode Island; Emiliani, B. (2020), *Irrational Institutions: Business, Its Leaders, and The Lean Movement*, Cubic LLC, South Kingstown, Rhode Island; Emiliani, B. (2020), *Management Mysterium: The Quest for Progress*, Cubic LLC, South Kingstown, Rhode Island; and Emiliani, B. (2022), *The Aesthetic Compass: Foundation of Leadership Action and Inaction*, Cubic LLC, South Kingstown, Rhode Island. For more information about these books, see https://bobemiliani. com/books/

[3] See, for example, the change in ownership at Twitter. Elon Musk's leadership undoubtedly acts as a retarding force on the advancement of leadership thinking and practice. Many top leaders view Musk's thinking and way of leading as a long-awaited return to an older, more traditional and less kind and supportive way of treating employees. For example, a CEO cannot force workers to work for free, but they can claim that employees are not working hard enough and demand that they work long hours or face dismissal. That is a way to force employees to work for free. What CEO would not want to get something for nothing? This reveals several

preconceptions about workers that are hallmarks of the ancient Institution of Leadership and the System of Profound Privilege (see Note 2). Borcher, C. (2022), "Is Elon Musk Your Boss's Anger Translator?," *The Wall Street Journal*, 22 November 2022, https://www.wsj.com/articles/is-elon-musk-your-bosss-an ger-translator-11669073893, accessed 22 November 2022 and Roose, K. (2022), "Elon Musk, Management Guru?," *The New York Times*, 16 December, https://www.nytimes.com /2022/12/16/technology/elon-musk-management-style.html, accessed 16 December 2022

[4] See "State of the Global Workplace: 2022 Report," https://www.gallup.com/workplace/349484/state-of-the-g lobal-workplace-2022-report.aspx and "The World's $7.8 Trillion Workplace Problem," https://www.gallup.com/ workplace/393497/world-trillion-workplace-problem.aspx, accessed 8 December 2022

[5] While it is an important topic, behavior change brought about by technology, such as cell phones, social media, or artificial intelligence, is not represented in this book.

[6] Leaders can be anyone from supervisor to CEO. In the present work, leaders are understood to be those in top leadership positions. That does not exclude the findings contained herein from applying to those in lower-level leadership positions.

[7] Or how chat bots such as OpenAIs ChatGPT could threaten Google's search engine business. "Google may be reluctant to deploy this new tech as a replacement for online

search, however, because it is not suited to delivering digital ads, which accounted for more than 80 percent of the company's revenue last year." Source: Grant, N. and Metz, C. (2022), "A New Chat Bot Is a 'Code Red' for Google's Search Business," *The New York Times*, 21 December. https://www.nytimes.com/2022/12/21/technology/ai-cha tgpt-google-search.html, accessed 21 December

[8] Consider a person who is serious about a home hobby that involves making and selling coffee tables. They are likely to be very motivated to improve their productivity to be able to produce coffee tables faster, at lower cost, with higher quality, and less struggle. They can do this because no barrier stands in the way of their ability to think and creatively solve such problems. No permission is necessary. Yet, when this same person goes to work, there may be little or no interest or motivation to improve their own work. They must get permission from managers to try out their ideas. In hierarchical organizations, productivity improvement is driven primarily by management, not by workers' own interests or desires. Managers typically hire workers to "do x," not "do x and improve how you do x." The clear message is "just do the job" or "follow the procedure." Managers get penalized by their bosses if workers don't do x or if improvement of x fails, which leads to risk avoidance by both workers and managers. This relates to a long-lived preconception – the anti-productivity "work intensification" argument invoked by union leaders and many sociologists who study labor – that the division of labor into unskilled or semi-skilled tasks and machine technology degrades and alienate workers from their work. It also relates to an ancient

preconception, leaders' denigration of productive labor to the lowest levels of status. Combined, these preconceptions mislead. It is, in fact, *hierarchy* that degrades and alienates workers from their work and disables workers' intrinsic desire to improve the productivity of their work. The consequence of the preconceptions about division of labor and machine technology is to maintain the status quo. Managers continue to drive workers and invest in machine technologies to improve productivity, workers continue to do as they are told, labor unions continue to fight with management, and labor researchers continue down a path that is unlikely to solve the problem because the problem itself is misunderstood. A change in preconception that it is hierarchy, not division of labor and machine technology that degrades and alienates workers from their work would break the status quo and lead to modifications in how hierarchies are understood (i.e., purpose and function) and lead to changes in how managers view people (e.g., motivated, creative), and how workers engage with their supervisor and work (e.g., rapport, teamwork, productivity, continuous improvement). It would also change manager's views on the scope and magnitude of investment needed for machine technologies. And it would change how labor leaders understand productivity and the details of contracts and substance of negotiations. This change in preconceptions can have profound effects on an organization and its stakeholders, but only if they are interested in something that is new and better. Alienation is not the sole province of workers. For leaders, their office-bound life leads to alienation from Nature, her finite resources, and negative externalities. It is a problem with astounding consequences.

Introduction

There has always been discontent among followers with how leaders behave, principally because they do not behave as followers expect, prefer, or believe brings about their best and most satisfying work [1]. This perpetual discontent leads to an obvious solution: change leadership behaviors. Changing leaders' behaviors is seen as the Holy Grail for better leadership. But what if it is not? What if that is a false hope? What if something much deeper produces the behaviors that followers dislike and wish to see changed?

From the perspective of leaders, most do not see changing their behaviors as being the necessity that followers think it is. And, generally, neither do leaders' peers [2]. As a group top leaders believe they are largely free to behave as they like and as situations dictate. They have earned the right to be unconstrained within certain limits of acceptability. And they do not comprehend leadership as a service to followers and other stakeholders. Thus, we have a large gap between what followers and leaders see as acceptable behaviors. The gap may close a little or a lot depending upon the leader. But overall, the gap is large and has existed for thousands of years [3].

Since the start of the study of leadership in the early 20th century [4], the focus has been on phenomena that are most easily observable: behaviors. Much work has been undertaken by many to understand leaders' behaviors and find methods and tools to improve their behaviors. Yet the consistent point of analysis is at the level of behaviors because behaviors are so obvious. The construct for this is:

Behaviors → Competencies

So, a given behavior will result in a given competency (skill or capability), be it good or bad. If you change the behavior, you get a different competency. For our interests, favorable new behaviors result in favorable new competencies of the kind that close the gap and thus please followers – the people who do the work.

Some people see it differently. Their construct is:

Process → Behaviors

Change the process (or system) to change behaviors. We know empirically that a change in process can have such an effect, we also know the effect can be short-lived. People will easily revert to the old process and associated behaviors [5].

In my early work on leadership, it seemed obvious that going from the current style of leadership to a new style of leadership was nothing more than a problem of changing one's behaviors [6]. All you have to do is specify new behaviors, tell leaders to practice the new behaviors, and *voilà!*, the new behaviors come into existence and followers are happy at long last. The construct:

Behaviors → Competencies

is commonly known as "leading by example." If the leader's

behaviors are bad, then other managers follow that example. If the leader's behaviors are good, then managers follow that example. What do we mean by "bad" leadership behaviors? It is this:

Greedy	Short-tempered
Abusive	Retaliates
Misleading	Overconfident
Manipulative	Disrespectful
Confrontational	Condescending
Bullying	Intimidating
Refuses to Listen	Autocratic
Belittles Others	Hypocrite
Publicly Humiliates	Political
Egotistical	Negative Attitude
Can't Admit Errors	Retaliates
Micromanaging	Inconsistent
Dishonest	Arrogant
Blames Others	Selfish
Inflexible	Intimidating
Disorganized	Indecisive

From many leaders' perspective, these are the behaviors – and many more like them – that get results. To have this view, leaders must ignore all the negative consequences that these behaviors have on the organization's daily collective efforts to satisfy customers. To the extent that they do so, they condone waste and chaos.

What do we mean by "good" leadership behaviors? It would be the antithesis of the above list, but in addition to that we can specifically say:

Respectful	Engaged
Humble	Helpful
Calm	Wise
Compassionate	Consistent
Inspirational	Patient
Generous	Humor
Reliable	Objective
Trusting	Observes
Listens	Shares Power
Reflects	Good Communicator
Honest	Balance
Fair	Open to Suggestions
Punctual	Clarifies Expectations

From many leaders' perspective, these are the behaviors that do not get results. Yet, other leaders see these good behaviors as precisely those that result in more efficient and effective functioning of the organization in its daily collective efforts to satisfy customers. This reflects an evolved perspective, typically based on personal experience, but not always so. These leaders see waste and chaos as unnecessary and as something that should be reduced or eliminated. In either case, it is leader's beliefs that produce the resulting behaviors. It then becomes apparent that the construct

$$\text{Behaviors} \rightarrow \text{Competencies}$$

is incorrect because leaders do not uniformly share the same beliefs. This is a fatal flaw of the once-popular "Competency

Model" method that emerged from the human resource and industrial psychology community [7]. The revised construct is as follows [8]:

Beliefs → Behaviors → Competencies

We will define "belief" as something accepted as true, usually untested; "behavior" as one's conduct based on beliefs; and "competency" as an established skill or capability. Remember, while we normally think of beliefs, behaviors, and competencies as something good, but they can also be bad. If you are good at doing something whose (often unintended) outcome is bad or wrong, that is referred to as "skilled incompetence" [9].

With the above construct we now have a logical sequence that helps us understand the direct connections between beliefs, behaviors, and competencies. Notice that leaders' beliefs are not something that is readily observable, unlike behaviors and competencies. We could stop here and be satisfied with having developed clear relationships between phenomena that are fact-based and can be deployed in leadership training. But think a little more and one would likely ask: "Where do leaders' beliefs come from?"

The next level down is preconceptions. The construct then becomes:

Preconceptions → Beliefs → Behaviors → Competencies

Now we have two levels of phenomena that are not readily

observable: preconceptions and beliefs. It is therefore not surprising that the simple construct,

$$\text{Behaviors} \rightarrow \text{Competencies}$$

is inadequate, if not wrong, to understand the truth of Jean-Baptiste Karr observation in relation to leadership and management:

"The more things change, the more they stay the same"

What, then, is a preconception? A preconception is variously defined as a preconceived opinion or idea *formed prior to experience*; a prejudice or bias; the *absence of reasoning* (Figure I-1). The italicized definitions are the most informative because they express the stealthy nature of preconceptions [10]. Preconceptions may or may not be misconceptions.

Figure I-1. AI generated (DALL·E 2) image depicting the absence of reasoning.

Where do preconceptions come from? They come from human experience and are absorbed through social learning processes that begin soon after birth. Preconceptions come from many different sources: parents, teachers, coaches, friends, family, bosses, co-workers, academics, priests, neighbors, doctors, books, television shows, magazines, newspapers, social media, videos, and so on, most of whom fulfill the role of "leader." For example, a boss at work imparts preconceptions about leadership and management prior to an employee's experience as a manager or leader, and likely in the *absence of reasoning*. The boss's preconceptions simply go unquestioned. Most of our preconceptions came from the experiences of other people prior to the day we were born, while a small number of preconceptions are artifacts of our own generation. Importantly, most preconceptions easily pass unaltered from one generation to another.

While it has been about 500 years since the reign of King Henry VIII, it has been only 17 generations from then to now, and only 67 generations from the time of Yeshua (Jesus Christ) to today. Thus, you can be assured that many of our preconceptions today come from that time and even much earlier times. Some of the preconceptions that we have absorbed since childhood have ancient origins, some have late-Medieval origins, and some are more recent. Importantly, the ways in which leaders think about people and business, whether Egyptian Queen or today's CEO, are similar in some ways and the same in other ways.

Here is a simple example of an exact way a King in prehistory and a CEO today share a preconception [11]. What do most

4

leaders do when problems arise in an organization? They blame one or more people for the problem. That is their behavior, driven by a preconception that it is both good and right to blame people for problems. This preconception probably dates from the start of the Holocene epoch some 12,000 years ago, a time when many different Deities were exalted or blamed for conditions beneficial or detrimental to human existence.

The hallmark of preconceptions is the *absence of reasoning*. Today's CEOs who blame people for problems today carry forward this *absence of reasoning* from prehistory. Reasoning, of course, would quickly reveal several important facts:

1. Most people are not malicious
2. Nobody likes to be blamed for problems
3. Most problems are caused by bad processes
4. Firing people does not eliminate process problems
5. Process problems can be corrected

These facts, if recognized by the CEO and accepted, would greatly improve the performance of the organization. Why, you may ask, is reasoning absent? In short, it is leaders' right and privilege to reason or not reason as they see fit, two of many entitlements constituted in the ancient Institution of Leadership (leaders' social habits of thought and action) and the System of Profound Privilege (the vested rights and interests that leaders protect and preserve) [12].

Humans have no way of avoiding the social learning process that infuses them with preconceptions and cannot go through life without them. Nor can humans spend their lives determining which preconceptions are beneficial, which are detrimental, and which are inconsequential. Preconceptions are an essential part of living. Yet they can interfere with a good life for self and others when preconceptions arouse internal or external conflict; e.g. racism, sexism, ageism, disability, religion, national origin, sexual orientation, economic insecurity, etc. As individuals we should be mindful of this and seek to understand ourselves so that we can avoid harming ourselves and others.

The situation is far more problematic for leaders at any level of an organization because they are responsible for the lives and livelihoods of other human beings. They should spend time giving thought to which of their many preconceptions are detrimental to their duties as leaders, to the lives and livelihood of employees, relationships with stakeholders, and to the efficient and effective functioning of the organization. This is especially true for top leaders. Yet, most of their preconceptions about people and business are socially constructed. To fit in with their peer group they must share the same preconceptions or risk being marginalized or ostracized. For most leaders, the consequences of this are too great to bear, and so it easier to align with the group's preconceptions even if the preconceptions are wrong, outdated, ineffective, or cause harm to other people or organizations. The *absence of reasoning* is an accepted form of thinking among leaders, used when and when needed. This, of course, drives employees mad. Hence, their calls for new behaviors. But what they should be calling for are new preconceptions, not new behaviors.

Here is another example. Many CEOs view suppliers as an enemy. Being far removed from actual interactions with suppliers, they imagine prices are too high and service is poor. They imagine all performance problems are solely the fault of suppliers and blame them for problems. That is their behavior, driven by a preconception that suppliers are deficient. CEOs are typically trained in root cause analysis, which always shows an effect is due to multiple causes, including causes generated by the company. But that cannot possibly be the case given the CEOs expert, error-free leadership. This, despite the reality that mutually beneficial relations between buyer and seller are possible and even desirable in terms of growth, prosperity, joint problem-solving, and responsiveness to changing market conditions. But, alas, adhering to preconceptions that helps define one's peer group is more important than the realization of "business excellence" that leaders persistently call for.

As tempting as it is to want to blame leaders for this problem, we must not do so because nearly everyone in a leadership position is affected by such preconceptions. The construct

Preconceptions → Beliefs → Behaviors → Competencies

shows that it is a process problem, not a people problem. This process problem is intertwined with the social learning process prior to work experience and during work experience, as well as the challenges associated with gaining and maintaining membership in good standing with one's in-group of leaders. Thus, for leaders, preconceptions are relatively fixed and constitute persistent, decades-long barriers to recognizing and achieving needed change. To make progress in how organizations are led and managed – to develop a changed perspective – the focus must be on process, not on people.

Huge sums of money are spent every year on behavior-based training and coaching for leaders at all levels. The training, grounded in psychological sciences, is fun and interesting and may not be substantially wrong. Yet the difficulty is that such training is unavoidably people-focused; meaning, its fundamental premise is that people are the problem. Psychologists generally to not recognize the processes that lead to what they comprehend as people problems. While some leaders respond positively to the training or coaching and incorporate it into their leadership routines, others have difficulty applying it to their job, while others are cynical and see such training as worthless. No matter what, such training often fails to have lasting effect. Those who find it beneficial often soon regress to prior behaviors due to:

- Occurrence or recurrence of serious business problems
- Continuing influence of one's own deeply rooted preconceptions
- In-group pressure to conform to preconceptions
- Circumstance where a display of toughness is judged to be required (shock effect)

Recall that the purpose of this book is to challenge the settled view – the common sense of the community, its deliberate socially and historically constructed body of thought – that better leadership is brought about simply by changing leaders' behaviors. The coming chapters will examine common leadership preconceptions in more detail, describe how they slow down or prevent needed progress, and how this leads to the difficult situations that leaders often find themselves in.

THINK

- Construct the tables below on a sheet of paper. Identify one or more leadership behaviors that results in a competency. Remember, the competency can something that is either good or bad. Make sure there is a logical connection between the items in each row (i.e., do not create two independent columns of lists).

Behavior → Competency

Behavior conduct based on beliefs	Competency established skill or capability

Next, figure out the belief that informs each behavior that you identified.

Belief → Behavior → Competency

Belief something accepted as true	Behavior conduct based on beliefs	Competency established skill or capability

Notes

[1] This includes things such as the meaning and purpose of work, personal development, fulfillment, work-home balance, health, prosperity, financial security, and well-being. Work beyond the hours for which workers are compensated and similar demands disrupt their personal or family life.

[2] Borcher, C. (2022), "Is Elon Musk Your Boss's Anger Translator?," *The Wall Street Journal*, 22 November 2022, https://www.wsj.com/articles/is-elon-musk-your-bosss-anger-translator-11669073893, accessed 22 November 2022 and Roose, K. (2022), "Elon Musk, Management Guru?," *The New York Times*, 16 December, https://www.nytimes.com/2022/12/16/technology/elon-musk-management-style.html, accessed 16 December 2022

[3] See Preface, Note 2, and Cooney, K. (2021), *The Good Kings: Absolute Power in Ancient Egypt and the Modern World*, National Geographic, Washington, D.C.

[4] Craig, D.R. and Charters, W.W. (1925), *Personal Leadership in Industry*, McGraw Hill Book Company, Inc., New York, New York

[5] Humans have a preference to process material and information using the batch-and-queue method. Some organizations change the process from old-style batch-and-queue to the new one-piece flow (i.e., process one item at a time, rather than processing items in large batches). However, left on their own, most workers will reverse the

improvement and return to the old way of working, batch-and-queue. Likewise, changes in management or changes in ownership will almost always result in a reversion to batch-and-queue processing. Batching has the convincing appearance of being less work. It is a form of hoarding and may be instinctive owing to the fear of not having what is needed when times are hard. This human survival instinct carries over into the workplace. The existence of corporate hierarchy (having a boss) reinforces the desire to batch to avoid getting yelled at – which is a form of "hard times" – for not having what is needed.

[6] Emiliani, M.L. (1998), "Lean Behaviors," *Management Decision*, Volume 36 Number 9, pp. 615- 631. https://doi.org/10.1108 /00251749810239504

[7] Lucia, A. and Lepsinger, R. (1999), *The Art and Science of Competency Models,* Jossey-Bass/Pfeiffer, San Francisco, CA

[8] Emiliani, M. (2003), "Linking Leaders' Beliefs to Their Behaviors and Competencies," *Management Decision*, Voume 41, Number 9, pp. 893-910, https://doi.org/10. 1108/00251740310497430 and Emiliani, M. and Stec, D. (2004), "Using Value Stream Maps to Improve Leadership," *Leadership and Organizational Development Journal*, Volume 25, Number 8, pp. 622-645, https://doi.org/10.1108/ 01437730410564979

[9] Argyris, C. (1986), "Skilled Incompetence," *Harvard Business Review*, September, https://hbr.org/1986/09/skilled -incompetence, Volume 9, September, pp. 74-79, accessed 22 November 2022

[10] Beliefs are not the same as preconceptions. Beliefs can be formed after experience and may be accompanied by reason. Preconceptions do not satisfy these criteria and are therefore different.

[11] One can easily imagine a King of Egypt blaming the head architect, engineer, and builder for building a lousy pyramid and for wasting resources. He would likely say something like: "I'm going to put your sarcophagus way out of town in a shitty little pyramid and make sure your dead-ass afterlife is fucking miserable!" It is more difficult to imagine the King saying: "Don't worry boys, you did your best. You'll get it right the next time. Now let's feast together!"

[12] The term "System of Profound Privilege" (Preface, Note 2) is a counterpoint to Dr. W. Edwards Deming's "System of Profound Knowledge." See Deming, W.E. (2000), *The New Economics for Industry, Government, Education*, Second Edition, Chapter 4, The MIT Press, Cambridge, Massachusetts, and https://deming.org/explore/sopk/, accessed 29 November 2022. See also "A Critique of the Learned Wisdom of Dr. Deming in Relation to the Worldly Wisdom of Business Leaders by Dr. Bob Emiliani," https://bobemiliani.com/wp-content/uploads/2022/06/Deming-vs-CM-2.pdf, accessed 29 November 2022

1

Preconceptions

When we interact with people in a business setting, we see most easily their behaviors and competencies. We say things like "Juan is easy to get along with" and "Samantha is good at coding." These are generally the two points of focus. What is less visible are the beliefs that inform the observed behaviors and competencies. We typically do not think much about someone's beliefs, likely assuming them to be more or less the same as our own. And we rarely question someone else's beliefs because doing so would be an infringement of their privacy. Consequently, beliefs remain largely hidden. They do, however, come up to the surface through spoken language (particularly rhetoric), written language, and by the decisions that leaders make. Most people do not observe at that level of detail. In an economic hierarchy such as business, the concern is directed towards doing a job, behaviors and competencies, rather than giving any deep thought to people's beliefs. It is much easier to assume that beliefs are the same or so similar that one need not bother thinking about it. Why, then, would anyone want to dig deeper to discover the preconceptions that inform beliefs? There seems to be no benefit in doing that.

Preconceptions are stealthy and mysterious because they are *formed prior to experience*. Being formed prior to experience instills confidence that experience is not necessary to confirm (or refute) preconceptions – hence, *an absence of reasoning*. For many of life's situations, preconceptions serve us well and help us lead a happy and full life. But for other life situations such as work, where we spend about one-third of our lives, preconceptions may not serve us as well as we think they do. They may in fact serve us very poorly, but we are likely unaware of that because everyone seems to have the same preconceptions. Humans rely on others' experiences, whether alive or dead, and devoid of context. And we assume they reasoned when they may not have because they too relied on the experiences of others before them. We readily absorb the life experiences of prior generations and take them as our own without having lived the experience. Without realizing it, we adopt the preconceptions handed down to us from influential people such as parents, teachers, bosses, etc., who in turn adopted the preconceptions handed down to them by prior generations.

This is where trouble begins. Problems of any type emanate from social and technical systems whose design is based on preconceptions of how things work or not work, or on how things should or should not work. This limits most people's desire to experiment and try new things. They see it as unnecessary because someone else long ago had the experience and did the reasoning, unaware that both may have been deeply flawed or valid only under narrow conditions or under conditions that have not existed for generations.

Take an activity such as production. Most systems are designed to produce physical items are "batch-and-queue" – producing items in large batches, with the items sitting it queue for long period of time before proceeding to the next step in the process. This method of processing likely dates to the dawn of agriculture 12,000 years ago, wherein crops were planted and harvested in batches. Agriculture was a huge advancement in providing the nutrients for life and whose surplus allowed people to make innovations in many new areas of human endeavor. Yet the breakthrough thinking from 400 generations ago remains with us today; most manufacturers still process material batch-and-queue, while many service businesses do the same, resulting in surplus.

An alternative method called "one-piece flow" [1] is counterintuitive and conflicts with human's ancient concern for survival (continuity). Yet, times have changed. We are 12,023 years past the dawn of agriculture, and one-piece flow production processes is a better way to make things in a resource constrained world because it consumes less resources. The problem of production remains with us today because of our preconceptions. This, in turn, drives beliefs that batch-and-queue is better, which leads to behaviors to design batch-and-queue systems and supporting subsystems, and then leads to competencies of building and operating batch-and-queue systems and related subsystems despite its limited utility in present times. And because huge knowledge and financial investments have been made in batch-and-queue processing over hundreds of generations, it continues along with such great force that one-piece flow is widely and swiftly rejected. That is the power of preconceptions, *formed prior to experience* and in the *absence of reasoning*.

Organizations are hierarchies wherein the top leader is in charge either by law, by right, or both. What the organization does or does not do depends on the top leaders' preconceptions in relation to changing conditions, as well as the preconceptions that direct reports share with the top leader. Top leaders tend to be conservative and risk averse and act in accordance with the wisdom [2]:

"What's next is most likely to be determined by what *is*."

Most leaders have a preconception that it is best for them to ensure continuity with the past; stability, statis, status quo; evolve slowly, if at all; control or suppress change, minimize change; maintain path dependence [3]. Consequently, organizations remain remarkably stable over the duration of their existence in terms of their social system [4], while technologies used or developed by organizations undergo change typically in continuity with past advances. Until such time as robots and AI fully appropriate the workplace, the functioning of an organization relies greatly on human thought and actions. Yet, there is a large gap between top leaders and workers in terms of the value of people and work. This gap is a fruitful realm for studying the preconceptions that guide leaders' thinking and actions and for explaining how and why leaders get embroiled in difficult situations.

But first, we must imagine the emergence of leaders in ancient society. It might go something like this [5]. Hundreds of thousands of years ago humans were engaged in a daily struggle for existence. That meant everyone working every day, men, women, and children buffeted by forces unknown, thus attributing good or bad fortune to magic and superstition. Over time, persons emerged as sorcerers with supernatural abilities, bestowed by Deities, connecting them to Nature and to life and death (e.g., rainmaking, fertility, healing, blessings, etc.). Accorded higher social status than those who lacked such capabilities, they made predictions and fulfilled requests for curing the ill, favorable weather, and abundance, and in doing so received many offerings. Priestly status exempted them from the daily work of survival needed in earlier times. The offerings led to wealth, the highest social status in the community, and power. As time passed, priests became kings. Their ascension to leader of the community meant that their words and conduct was beyond reproach. As king or queen anointed by Deities, their viewpoints, words, ideas, and wisdom became sacrosanct and evolved to become the common sense of the community, subtended by ancient myths, magic, and superstition. It became accepted *without prior experience* and in the *absence of reasoning* because the leader's words are, by the grace of the Deities, sacred and must be taken by all as fact. Those who question or criticize the leader are destined to face dire consequences. There is no need for experience or reasoning; simply listen to the top leader and think as they do and do as they say.

Time passes and people start to think for themselves. They come to see top leaders as not so mighty, not so magical, not descended from God, and subject to criticism. Yet, over hundreds of generations, the preconceptions have been locked into place. Even though divine right is no longer associated with top leaders, they believe themselves to be substantively different than the workers. They are correct; top leaders are substantively different from others. They are both members and keepers of the ancient Institution of

Leadership and the System of Profound Privilege; the Institution of Leadership being comprised of the foundational elements that produce a way of thinking that typically goes unrecognized and unchallenged by leaders, while the System of Profound Privilege comprises the unearned authority, freedom, entitlements, advantages, opportunities, rights, benefits, and immunities from liability enjoyed by those with the highest social status. Consequently, there remains a large gap in status between leaders and followers that sustains ancient preconceptions to this day and will likely continue well into the future due to path dependence. So, what are the preconceptions of those who lead organizations, particularly businesses? We begin with an enumeration of Foundational Preconceptions whose function is to restrict or thwart change.

Foundational Preconceptions

- Whatever is, is right
- Humans have limitations
- Repress enthusiasm
- Support and defend the status quo
- Trial and error is not a plan
- Respect traditions
- Logic is slow and laborious
- Reason ignores real-world constraints
- Adapt gradually and judiciously
- It works, don't experiment
- Scientific thinking is hazardous
- Place restrictions on things

- Continuous change destabilizes
- Avoid abstract schemes
- Imagination disappoints
- Alternatives are worse
- Instinct and intuition are more useful than facts
- Things cannot be perfected
- Conflict and competition are desirable
- Hierarchical control
- Proceed cautiously
- Revere institutions
- Omniscience

These preconceptions illustrate the point made earlier, that leaders' preconceptions serve the purpose of ensuring continuity with the past, maintaining the status quo, suppressing change, or minimizing change if change must occur. The preconceptions listed result in beliefs, behaviors, and competencies that ensure change perpetually lags the needs of society, whether it is social or technological change – with social lag being much greater than technological lag.

Each item on the list can be *formed prior to experience* and a reflects an *absence of reasoning*. We hear, read, or witness these or similar things from our top leaders. Because of their high status, coupled with our ancient preconception that leaders, descended from Deities, know more than we do and are smarter than we are, we readily absorb their preconceptions, believe what they believe, behave as they behave, and seek their competencies. In doing so, we generally fail to think for ourselves. Our abilities to reason are suspended. As each new generation of leadership ascends to the top they think and do things as prior generations did. From the perspective of the ancient Institution of Leadership and the System of Profound Privilege, this is as it should be. Tradition is preserved; hierarchical control is preserved; the Institution of Leadership and System of Profound Privilege, in existence for 12,000 years or more, survives. Natural order is preserved.

Or so it seems. Humans as a species are curious and creative, bursting with ideas and a desire to experiment and try new things that have the possibility of improving human existence. Restraining that instinct is unnatural. It limits choices, agency, collaboration, productivity, innovation, and progress. Further, Nature is not all-giving of her resources. She has limits which leaders' varied preconceptions – economic, social, political, historical, philosophical, spiritual, aesthetic, technological, and legal – do not permit fully acknowledging. If one were to dispense with the idea of leaders descending from Deities, then the constellation of preconceptions would be substantially different and likely better for the long-term survival of humanity. It is through the artifice of sorcery and conflict (war) that status arises and makes it difficult for humans, whether at the top or the bottom of the hierarchy, to think for themselves.

Artificial intelligence lies within humans. Preconceptions are a type of artificial intelligence algorithm that initiates and sustains opinions and ideas *formed prior to experience* and *absent of reasoning*. Thus, we inadvertently forgo human intelligence: sensing, awareness, understanding, caring, concern, logic, abstract thinking, judgment (moral, ethical, aesthetic, etc.), cause-and-effect, and so on [6]. As a result, humanity has difficulty learning and adapting concurrently with changing conditions. While there is ample evidence from personal and group experience to refute the Foundational Preconceptions listed on the previous pages, the intangible artifact of human existence, status, exerts a formidable retarding force on the process of change whether in business or society, and calls into question leaders' objectivity. Their preconceptions signal a particular socio-economic condition that favors leaders' interests above all others. It also leads to complacency.

Humans are problem-solvers. When we do not understand how something works, we try to figure it out. In hierarchies, such efforts are often frowned upon by leaders. They prefer that workers just do their job. This leaves a void in leaders' understanding, one that gets filled by preconceptions. In a classic test, people asked to draw a bicycle from memory created such poor renderings that, if made, the bicycles would not work. This reveals a preconception that we think we can easily understand how things work, even something as simple as a bicycle. But most of us fail at that. What about more complex things such as a hand mixer, oven, computer, software, automobile, airplane, or a business and its internal and external (customer and supplier) processes? Surely, we would do much worse.

If we are honest about our lack of understanding of how most things work, and unafraid of what others will think of us, we would say, "It's magic!" or "It's the work of magicians." Of course, we clearly understand these things to be human creations. But as the artifacts of human existence become more complex and locked in the black boxes of advanced information technologies, we move closer to what we once were in our evolutionary history: people who attributed existence – life and death, abundance and scarcity, success and failure, innovation and stagnation, pleasure and pain – to magic and Gods. In this sense, our collective ancient spirituality could reassert itself and become a significant force in future human thought and action.

Let's now turn our attention to leaders' preconceptions, those that are particularly significant in organizational settings, and make them explicit as objects for analysis and possible revision – again recognizing that preconceptions are predominately noncognitive and gained through social learning. Categorically, the preconceptions are: Economic, Social, Political, and Historical. As with the previous list, this and following lists of preconceptions are not intended to be comprehensive. Rather, they illustrate the point that that better leadership is not brought about simply by changing leaders' behaviors, and to further show how preconceptions guide leaders' thinking and actions and explain how and why difficult situations arise.

Economic Preconceptions

- Natural rights
- Self-interest
- Invisible hand
- Free markets
- Efficient markets
- Manage with measures

- Workers paid too much
- Shareholder supremacy
- Growth
- Regulation increases costs
- Economies of scale
- Automation
- Short-term focus [7]
- Zero-sum outcomes
- Debt and leverage are good
- Labor cost focus
- Unit cost and unit price focus
- Incalculable costs do not exist
- Supply driven, sellers' market view
- Batch-and-queue processing
- Outsourcing lowers costs
- Economic order quantities
- Budget cutting is cost cutting
- Business as a game or battle

Review the list and tickmark the economic preconceptions that stand out as being the most effective at holding back social or technological progress in your workplace.

Social Preconceptions

- Natural order
- Leaders lead, workers work
- Respect is not bilateral
- Leaders smart and heroic, workers dumb

- People are the problem
- Do not trust workers
- Workers don't want to work
- Workers don't work hard enough
- Problems are bad
- Blame people for problems
- Individualism over teamwork
- Laborers do only labor
- Workers serve leaders
- Others need to change, not leaders
- In-groups and out-groups
- Can be selfish and unfair
- Ignore feedback from stakeholders
- Doing harm does no harm
- Conflict has zero cost

Review the list and tickmark the social preconceptions that stand out as being the most effective at holding back social or technological progress in your workplace.

Political Preconceptions

- Leadership self-interest
- Company comes first
- Don't question authority
- Business principles are not necessary
- Bureaucracy is strength
- One best way
- Organizational politics

- Winning
- Authority trumps scientific thinking
- Promotion based on loyalty
- Machine technology solves all problems
- Ignore stakeholders
- Unions, labor, suppliers are bad
- Business is business
- Waste is a feature, not a bug

Review the list and tickmark the political preconceptions that stand out as being the most effective at holding back social or technological progress in your workplace.

Historical Preconceptions

- Divine right
- Infallibility
- Maintain the status quo
- Don't question the leader
- Loyalty
- Status and prestige
- Conflict
- Linear thinking, not systems thinking
- Results more important than process
- Preference for quick wins and shortcuts
- Need doers, not thinkers
- Abundance

Review the list and tickmark the historical preconceptions that stand out as being the most effective at holding back social or technological progress in your workplace.

These preconceptions can cross categories and there may be relations between preconceptions in different categories. In other words, the system of preconceptions is complex and interrelated (Figure 1-1). Further, one can easily add other categories of preconceptions such as philosophical, spiritual, aesthetic, technological, and legal. The five categories presented will suffice to make case that better leadership is not brought about simply by changing leaders' behaviors because the underlying preconceptions are so numerous and remain largely intact. It also establishes the groundwork for understanding how leaders so often find themselves in complex and chaotic situations.

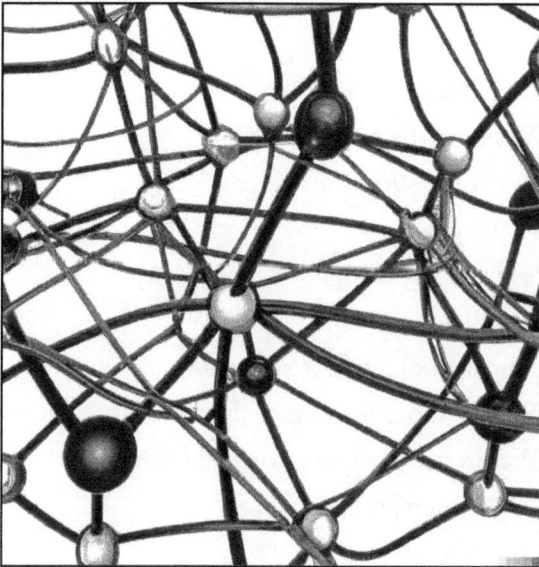

Figure 1-1. AI generated (DALL·E 2) image depicting an interconnected network of preconceptions.

The preconceptions, invariably taken as axiomatic, largely, but not completely, define the "common sense" of the community of top leaders that I describe as the Institution of Leadership and System of Profound Privilege. They map the "common sense" of leaders that inform their beliefs, behaviors, and competencies, and endure because they easily adapt to changing times. They reflect the enduring rights and privileges bestowed upon leaders by ancient rights or Deities, and they capture the unique leadership culture and way of thinking refined over several millennia. They reflect culturally formed truths, not absolute truths. Because the preconceptions have been sanctified, leaders continuously bend those lower in the hierarchy to their ways of thinking overtly, in skillfully subtle ways, and perhaps even unconsciously. This legitimizes both the function and power of leadership and thus serves leaders' interests, which in their view also rightly serves the larger community's interests. But there are two problems with that:

- Most of the preconceptions fit with a long-gone past that does not exist today, and thus no longer serve the community's interests.

The effect is to maintain continuity with the long-ago past. The good of the community today differs from the good of the community 500, 5000, or 12000 years ago. The continuing application of these preconceptions illustrates the point: "You can make change without progress, but you can't make progress without change" [8]. Submission to leaders' preconceptions and associated mythologies leads to a perpetual fandom that mistakes change for progress.

- The preconceptions are both the source of difficult problems and the informant of leaders' solutions to difficult problems.

Leaders, being far removed from those lower in the hierarchy, lack the specialized technical knowledge that workers possess. Their only frame of reference for work processes are their preconceptions. This leads to the complex and chaotic problems that leaders must contend with, whose only solutions lie within the same preconceptual frame of reference. The common sense – the social habits of thought and action – used by leaders assures inadequacy of problem-solving, repetition of errors [8], and eventual destabilization of the organization. This often leads to a change in leadership, and the cycle begins anew. Top leaders are keenly observant of the limitations and failings of others. However, they cannot see how their preconceptions generate difficult problems and how their preconceptions inform solutions to difficult problems that are inadequate.

Leaders' preconceptions are dangerous in the sense that they preclude listening to the forewarnings of problems presented by low-level workers or managers [10], as well as their proposed solutions to problems. Leaders become trapped by the common sense of the Institution of Leadership, rooted in the dead hand of the past [11]. Inevitably, and according to the preconceptions that inform the common sense of leaders and the Institution of Leadership, the people lower in the hierarchy suffer the consequences of leader's mistakes. The viewpoint informed by leaders' preconceptions, "whatever is, is right," prevents the type of problem-solving that is needed to make progress [12]; i.e., observation, facts, and truth.

While under these conditions there has been some 350 years of expanding global financial and material prosperity, the focus of the next 350 years may need to shift to human survival and the habitability of Earth [13, 14], which calls for a different set of leadership preconceptions. Even if this shift does not come to pass, it seems clear that leaders' current preconceptions do not reflect the shared interests of the community and are not suitable for the continued social advancement of humanity.

THINK

- Identify other Foundational Preconceptions.

- Construct the table below on a sheet of paper. Complete the sequence beginning for several preconceptions. Make sure there is a logical connection between the items in each row (i.e., do not create two independent columns of lists).

Preconception → Belief → Behavior → Competency

Preconception prior to experience, absence of reasoning	Belief something accepted as true	Behavior conduct based on beliefs	Competency established skill or capability

- Identify other Economic Preconceptions.

THINK

- Identify other Social Preconceptions.

- Identify other Political Preconceptions.

- Identify other Historical Preconceptions.

Notes

[1] See Sekine, K. (1992), *One-Piece Flow: Cell Design for Transforming the Production Process*, Productivity Press, Portland, Oregon and Protzman, C. McNamara, J., Protzman, D. (2015), *One-Piece Flow vs. Batching: A Guide to Understanding How Continuous Flow Maximizes Productivity and Customer Value*, Productivity Press, New York, New York

[2] Dowd, D. (1958), *Thorstein Veblen*, Cornell University Press, Ithaca, New York, p. 157

[3] Emiliani, B. (2022), *The Aesthetic Compass: Foundation of Leadership Action and Inaction*, Cubic LLC, South Kingstown, Rhode Island

[4] Hence, leader's distaste for work from home (WFH), "quiet quitting," doing only what is required within the bounds of an eight-hour day (i.e., reduction in free labor and worker's desire to have a life), demands for higher pay and better working conditions, and related workplace phenomena brought about by the COVID-19 pandemic, inflation, the steadily declining wealth of the middle class, growth of the paycheck-to-paycheck class, etc. These changes are seen by most leaders as an undesirable loss of control; changes in the workplace that are not on their terms.

[5] Frazer, J.G. (1905), *Lectures on the Early History of the Kingship*, Macmillan and Co., Limited, London, United Kingdom

[6] While artificial intelligence is on the verge of being able to reason as humans do, it cannot yet experience life as humans do. Experience gives humans a significant edge in comprehending the common sense of the community, sensing, caring, ethics, and causal relationships. On the other hand, experience can be overrated because it can solidify into place varied preconceptions that retard or prevent progress (i.e., innovations in science, technology, society, etc.). Artificial intelligence seems problematic from the standpoint that its base of knowledge is human experience comprising the interconnected network of archaic preconceptions. Serving up archaic preconceptions for the foreseeable future will likely retard human progress. Will AI instead somehow learn the limitations of these preconceptions? Will it advise us which old preconceptions to abandon and which new ones we should take up? What will be AIs rationale for making such determinations? How will AIs common sense evolve; along with society or instead of it? Can you trust it?

[7] One must be cautious with the words "short-term focus" because unlike the other preconceptions, it is fundamental to the nature of business to be short-term, i.e., do today what needs to be done today, worry about tomorrow when it arrives. Difficulties arise when the mid- and long-term are consistently sacrificed by leaders to achieve short-term gains.

[8] Source: Mark Harari, 2022

[9] For a thorough categorization and enumeration of leaders' repetitive errors, please see Emiliani, B. (2015), *Speed Leadership: A New Way to Lead for Rapidly Changing Times*, The

CLBM LLC, Wethersfield, Connecticut

[10] Many complex corporate problems could have been averted had senior leaders listened to low-level workers and managers. For example, Boeing's 737 Max disasters, Wells Fargo corporate fraud, BPs Deepwater Horizon disaster, Morandi Bridge disaster, and so on. The list is long, sad, and dishonorable. See Emiliani, B. and Torinesi, M. (2021), *Wheel of Fortune: Getting to the Heart of Business Strategy*, Cubic LLC, South Kingstown, Rhode Island

[11] There is a type of "unnatural selection" that involves the preservation (survival) of favored preconceptions, not those that are most desirable or needed as social conditions change (i.e., evolution). The current environment is one in which it is defined by the needs of leaders more than the needs of society, and which accepts these preconceptions as final. The survival of leaders' preconceptions over centuries and longer confirms their value to leaders, which limits change and raises the energy required for change which is itself constrained by archaic preconceptions. As such, leaders' sense-making is heavily reliant on traditions, myths, superstitions, legends (glory; i.e., spiritual transcendence), and the like. These are employed as valuable commodities to sell and are eagerly purchased by followers hoping to gain elevated status (and protection). This leads to status quo, contrary to the facts of ever-changing social, technological, and ecological environments. This book seeks to make the case that preconceptions should change from those best adapted to the current environment defined by the needs of leaders (guided by a preconception of abundance and a quest for

evermore) to those that are most desirable or needed for human survival and sustainability of the habitat.

[12] Archaic preconceptions can be thought of as a type of colonialism. As such, it is a low-information system in terms of human-to-human communication, which suppresses or ignores problems – especially when workers are assumed to be disloyal and inefficient.

[13] War within and between nations, being environmentally ruinous, comprises preconceptions that by now must be considered archaic and replaced with preconceptions that facilitate Earthcare and related entrepreneurship.

[14] For a very interesting and consequential emerging battle of preconceptions, see "It's Time to Quit Capitalism's Obsession with Growth. Focus on 'Degrowth' Instead," by David Meyer, *Fortune*, 22 December 2022, https://fortune .com/2022/12/22/degrowth-economic-growth-recession-k ohei-saito, accessed 22 December 2022

2

Dead Hand of the Past

The preconceptions listed in Chapter 1 largely, but not completely, define the metaphysical foundation of the ancient Institution of Leadership and System of Profound Privilege. What do we mean by metaphysical? It is the claim of a reality, or of the nature of reality, that is external to sense perception; self-evident truths; that which is beyond reason; an idea or doctrine that transcends causation and is scientifically unverifiable; e.g., Divine right. Preconceptions are "first principles" (*ab initio*, "from the beginning"), the fundamental propositions that cannot be deduced from any other proposition.

At its root, leadership of the type commonly found in organizations is an ancient Deistic philosophy, one that embraces Natural Law and Natural Order [1]. Given that as its foundation, it is plain to see that the dead hand of the past remains the unseen force that guides leadership thinking and practice. In many cases, this is not a problem of special interest. It may even be beneficial to the advancement of humanity. But in other cases, the dead hand of the past functions as a force that retards progress. Is retarding progress always a bad thing? If so, how do you know?

Let's begin with the questions: "What is progress?" and "When is progress is needed?" Progress, in the context of this book, means the advancement of material well-being; a change that elevates human interests or humanity to a higher level; an improvement; moving forward versus remaining in place or regressing; survival. Progress is change that most people would recognize as beneficial, though at times it is not always better. There is no doubt that progress can be highly contentious. People can formulate many reasons for or against progress, not fully realizing the grander implications of either. But with certainty we can say that humanity has progressed over time – the ends being undefined – and that most people would view that favorably due to improvement in material well-being. But for some it is a source of conflict with respect to spiritual (not necessarily religious) well-being, which generates resistance to progress.

When is progress needed? Usually, when problems arise, when people come up with ideas to try directed towards improvement, or when individuals or society undergo a change in sentiment about their lives or livelihoods. Given that existence has no choice but to confront continuous change, it must also confront continuous problems. That, in turn, propels people, individually and in total, towards continuous improvement as the solution to the problem of continuous change. But are they successful?

Over the long arc of time there appears to be a meliorative trend in all material aspects of human existence [2], whose end is undefined. But what about leadership, a social aspect of human existence? One can imagine, or read historical accounts, of business leaders' – monarchies as well as those engaged in private commerce – overt barbarism. In the so-called developed world, barbarism of the type that existed in both the distant and recent past seems to be extinct. Yet most of the Foundational Preconceptions that informed leaders' barbarism then remain with us today. So, is there a meliorative trend in leadership, or have leaders past overt barbarism simply become covert and more mental (stress) than physical (blood, sweat) in its focus? If it is the latter, then we can conclude that the Deistic metaphysical foundation of leadership remains in force today and that a meliorative trend towards benevolent or servant leadership as a final state does not exist, as many people hope it does.

The role of leadership is conceived in self-regarding terms as a natural, harmonious state of existence for all living things for all time. Therefore, leadership as a practice lacks a scientific basis – the aforementioned *absence of reason*. And leadership as an academic field of inquiry lacks a scientific basis because it uncritically accepts the preconceptions listed in Chapter 1 as the starting point of inquiry. In other words, it does not question the metaphysical foundation of the Institution of Leadership and System of Profound Privilege, therefore it interferes with scientific analysis and undermines the accuracy and utility of the causal relationships under study. Consequently, leadership problems do not actually get solved despite the sustained efforts of academics, consultants, and many others, and so leadership itself does not evolve over time as one would expect.

Why is leadership not evolutionary? Why don't the preconceptions, the metaphysical foundations of leadership, change over time in ways that are closer to being in-step with follower's wants and needs. Why is leadership pre-Darwinian, frozen with preconceptions that should have been altered or eliminated as time passed? After all, leadership is enmeshed in society, not separate from it. Society progresses, but leadership, overall, does not, and most of society's progress is technological for which leaders (owners of technology) are happy to sponsor, owing to its profitability or prestige, though always doing so on their terms. Furthermore, technological progress means material progress, which is a highly effective balm that soothes and distracts individuals and society from leadership deficiencies and failures. This is a more elegant and refined way to sustain the Institution of Leadership and System of Profound Privilege compared to earlier times.

If leadership were post-Darwinian, adaptive, it would lie on a different metaphysical foundation of preconceptions that align better, though not perfectly, with the humanistic, fact-based, cause-and-effect reality of the material world. Alignment is imperfect because faith, no matter how small or alien to one's thinking, accompanies reason whether one likes it or not. Leadership on Darwinian grounds would be a process of change approximately in step with the changing social environment to which it is part of. It would come under the actual dynamic forces at work rather than remain under the static ancient Deistic philosophy. It would reverse the myth of command-and-control as the preferred way to lead people. As an evolutionary process, the end state of leadership is indeterminate. It could evolve into varied forms of servant or communitarian leadership, it could be replaced by autonomous teams guided by disinterested facilitators, or it could disappear altogether because it's function and status claims no longer contribute to survival.

What seems clear is that followers' discontent with leadership is not corrected by behavior-based training. While it is true that such training is fun and interesting and does help some leaders improve – and it could be grounded in good science or the appearance of good science – it does not solve problems or meet needs. Leaders are extraordinarily adept at saying right things and behaving in right ways when needed, but the underlying preconceptions remain solidly in place. Even major life experiences, such as newsworthy company bankruptcies or product failures, do not usually compel top leaders to question their preconceptions.

Leadership must move from a metaphysical ground of meeting its own needs to a metaphysical ground that recognizes the whole of human experience and thus move forward with scientific discovery and new ideas to try. The objective is to close the gap between current reality and the ancient preconceptions, the burden of history, possessed by the people charged with leading people and organizations. The required mental adaptation can come from within, but a wider scope of change in leadership thinking and action will come from the environment once it is recognized that circumstances have changed beyond that which can continue to sustain the metaphysical foundation of the ancient Institution of Leadership and System of Profound Privilege. The COVID-19 pandemic is one such example. It is likewise an example of regression, partial or full, to prior preconceptions once the pandemic is perceived by leaders to be over [3].

As one climbs the hierarchy under the present set of

Leadership preconceptions, there is a devolution, negative adaptation, in preconceptions from current-day material preconceptions to ancient metaphysical preconceptions. These preconceptions are self-reinforcing due to the requirement to emulate one's peers as one attains higher social status. The preconceptions become emulative standards for comparison, and their existence becomes evident in the homogeneous engineered language and rhetoric that leaders use among themselves and in the course of their daily duties. The preconceptions and associated language, including business idioms and clichés, generate a self-authenticating version of reality that resists change. Whatever information or problem that does not lie within the accepted language is seen as less important or part of a reality that does not exist (e.g., workers' problems, workers' reality), and which meets with leaders' disapproval giving them grounds for dismissing it. Under such conditions where facts are inconvenient or irrelevant, the deep commitment to ancient preconceptions – devotion, absence of doubt, and *absence of reason* – takes on a spiritual form that multiplies the difficulty of replacing them.

Were it solely a matter of facts, change might be easier. But there are two significant impediments:

- Acquisition and maintenance of status
- Spiritual commitment to the Institution of Leadership and System of Profound Privilege

These impediments subvert learning and evolution in leadership preconceptions that would lead to different thinking and practices. Figure 2-1 is an adaptation of Michael Porter's "Five Forces" framework for analyzing power in business competition [4] applied to analyzing power and competition between workers and business leaders for making progress (i.e., keeping up with the times). In this representation [5], the progressive, productive, and evolutionary work of employees represent threats to leaders' status quo which activates a spiritual call to arms to fend off threats. In this framework, "good" leadership is one that withstands threats of efficiency, improvement, creativity, and social change, and which is also strongly teleological (deterministic, nonevolutionary) – the combination of which

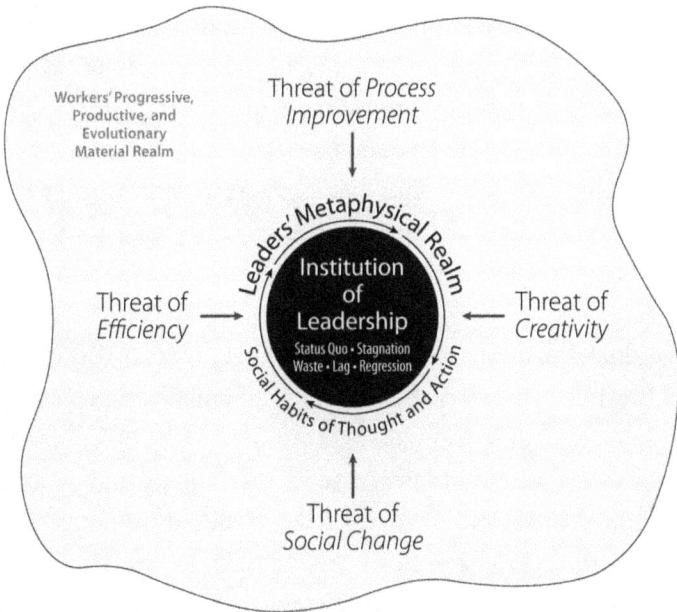

Figure 2-1. Framework analyzing competition between workers and business leaders for making progress. Adapted from Porter [4].

reflects self-regarding proclivities. Like Porter's "Five Forces" framework, Figure 2-1 also affects the ability of the company to serve its customers and make a profit.

Of course, the dichotomy that exists in most organizations is that workers are focused on running processes and serving customers (other-regarding proclivities) while leaders are focused on running the business and making profits (self-regarding proclivities). The latter proclivities are seen by leaders as being far superior to the former. Consequently, management decisions are often counterproductive in relation to serving customers interests. Likewise, management decisions are often counterproductive to continuously improving corporate culture, to the ability to execute strategy, and for keeping up with the times. Within the confines of the Institution of Leadership, there is great competition for top leadership positions, but little or no competition for leadership ideology. Ascension through the ranks necessarily culls the candidates who wish to see the current leadership ideology replaced with a new ideology.

In addition to a threats-based framework, we can also look at this from the standpoint of learning. Figure 2-2a depicts the single- and double-loop learning models for people engaged in some real-world activity that involves goals and requires decision-making. Notice that I have modified the single-loop learning model to be exclusive to workers, salaried or hourly. The significance of this modification will become apparent when we discuss the learning models for top leaders. Single-loop learning (top of Figure 2-2a) begins with a mental model, a set of preconceptions, that informs rules for

Single-Loop Learning
for Workers

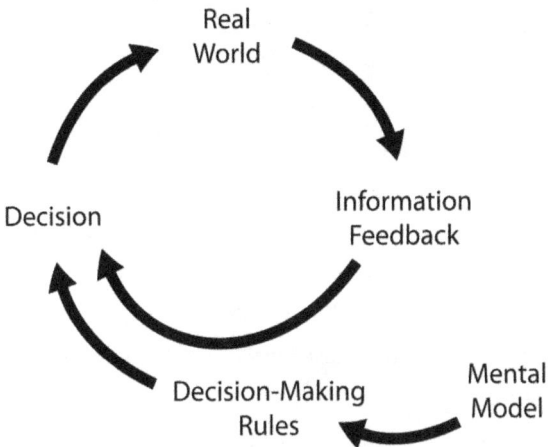

Real
World

Information
Feedback

Decision

Decision-Making
Rules

Mental
Model

Double-Loop Learning
for Workers

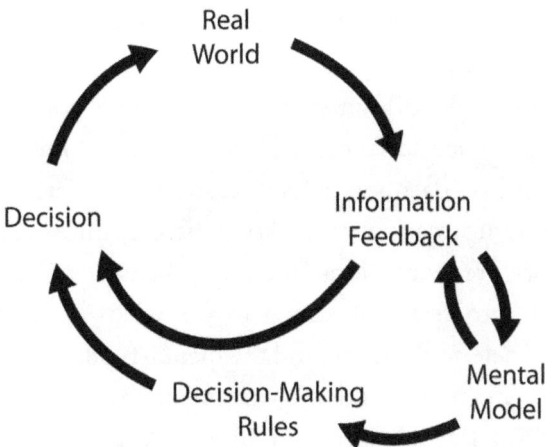

Real
World

Information
Feedback

Decision

Decision-Making
Rules

Mental
Model

Figure 2-2a. Single- and double-loop learning for workers [6].

decision-making. A decision is made that generates some real-world result which then produces feedback that may become relevant to some future decision. Single-loop learning does not use feedback to question the mental model on which decisions are based. Nor does it question the goal or method. The outcome is to restrict learning to the realm of the mental model, to defend decisions and the mental model upon which decisions are made, thus maintaining the status quo. In Double-loop learning (bottom of Figure 2-2a), the information feedback leads to questions (e.g., "Why are we doing it that way?") that result in changes to the mental model – changes to the set of preconceptions – that changes decision-making rules, goals, and methods for future decisions. The outcome is progress.

The situation is different for top leaders [7]. They are not in the "real world" that workers occupy (as Argyris and Schön assumed [6]). Leaders are far removed from the real world, the material world that low-level employees are engage with to make and deliver goods and services to customers. For leaders, the real world in single-loop learning (top of Figure 2-2b) is bypassed in favor of leaders' metaphysical world of metrics, KPIs, dashboards, spreadsheets, money, third- or fifth-hand information, etc., all of which are informed by the leadership preconceptions cited in Chapter 1. Again, the outcome is to restrict learning to the realm of the mental model, to defend decisions and the mental model upon which decisions are made, and thus maintain the status quo. In double-loop learning (bottom of Figure 2-2b), the leader engages both the metaphysical world of metrics, KPIs, etc., and material world, as these two worlds are connected.

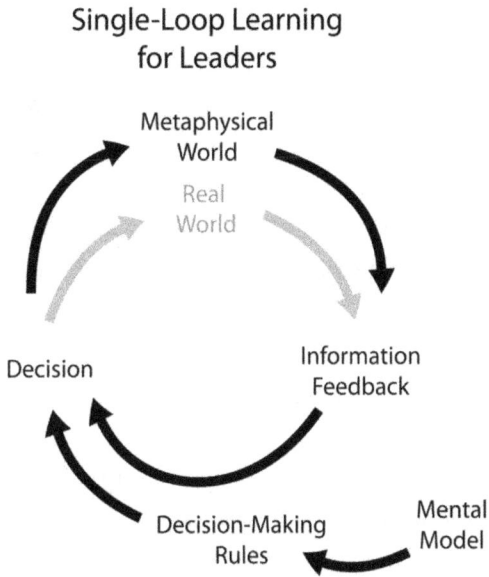

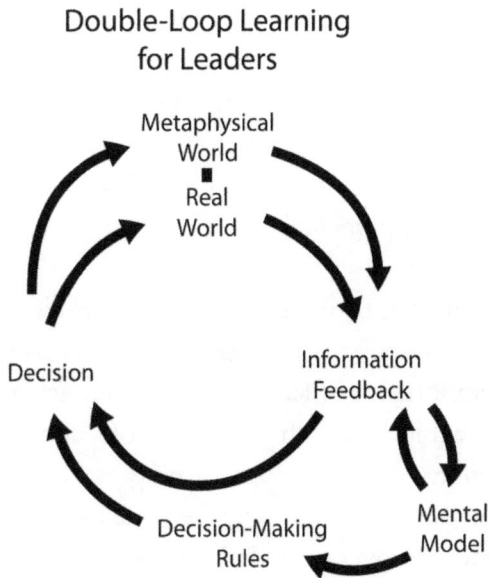

Figure 2-2b. Single- and double-loop learning for leaders [6, 7].

This provides much higher levels of information feedback; more accurate acquisition and clearer comprehension of the facts. And it results in changes to the mental model – changes to the set of preconceptions – that changes goals, methods, and decision-making rules for future decisions [8]. The outcome is to break the status quo – whose justification is tradition and Divine right, not reason, function, or need – and make progress.

Yet very few leaders engage in double-loop learning (bottom of Figure 2-2b) due to the supremacy of the mental model (leadership preconceptions, Chapter 1) in which status and spiritual commitment to the Institution of Leadership and System of Profound Privilege are sacrosanct. As a result, most leaders are loath to engage the real world, preferring instead to lead from the office, informed by metaphysical representations of the real world (metrics, KPIs, etc.). This avoids the diminution of status and spiritual commitment that occurs with double-loop learning, but it succeeds in making life difficult for all other stakeholders, society, and the planet due to perpetual lag.

The significance of Figure 2-2b is that most leaders are single-loop learners despite the profusion of interviews where they claim the importance of learning. What they actually mean is learning within the framework of long-established preconceptions. Double-loop learning is the ground for questioning the status quo, activities, goals, etc., and thus for making new discoveries and developing higher grades of learning that result in progress in leadership and management practice.

We face many critical questions today with respect to work, life, business, government, society, and the planet. The continuing dominance of single-loop learning among leaders, surely mirrored by followers and a primary source of conflict among those who don't, suggests that humanity may not be up to the task of responding to these critical questions [9]. In other words, in societies driven by pecuniary interests whose reward is wealth and power (ancient preconceptions), double-loop learning seems a thoroughly foolish thing to do. But if interests shift to human survival and improving the human habitat and human experience, then double-loop learning is both brilliant and indispensable [10].

Yet we are not on a trajectory of double-loop learning among top leaders; business or political leaders. If preconceptions do not get modified as a result of experience, feedback, and reflection, then decision-making becomes increasingly out of step with both the times and human needs. Leaders keep people, organizations, and society stuck in the past when present conditions call for something different. Decisions become increasingly irrational in relation to what is actually needed as determined by individuals, society, or the biosphere.

Figure 2-3 illustrates the problem. If generation after generation of leader remains committed to the preconceptions listed in Chapter 1 – committed to the traditional metaphysical foundation – then a succession of problems is solved using evermore irrational solutions resulting in ever-greater complexity that becomes more difficult to disentangle. These solutions are readily formed or copied by other leaders because they comprise the common sense of the Institution of Leadership and System of Profound Privilege.

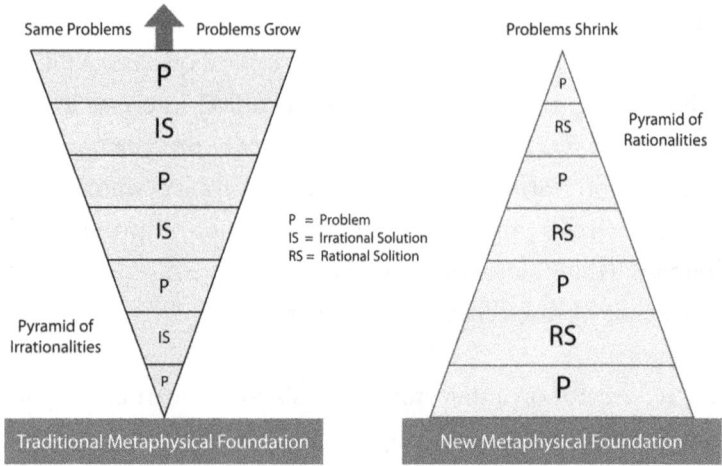

Figure 2-3. Pyramids of irrationality and rationality.

Leaders become manufacturers of complex and chaotic problems that lead to confusion, instead of problem-solvers. This normalizes irrationality, which leaders readily copy from one another, thus eliminating the human mind as a purposive agent capable of learning and improvement [11]. For example, when a problem arises, it is nearly always a people problem, not a process problem. Sooner or later, this results in a destabilization of the organization (or society), which disturbs ideation and innovation. Both leaders and followers can agree that such an outcome would be undesirable.

An alternative is double-loop learning so that problems get solved with solutions that are more rational to avoid instabilities of the type that cause harm to people and planet. This must not be construed as advocacy for pure rationality. Such a thing cannot exist and would generally be unwise. But consider that leaders have long had concerns about logical, rational scientific thinking (facts, cause-and-effect, etc.) having perverse effects on leadership and management. Yet, there is substantially no concern about the perverse effects of irrational or archaic preconceptions on leadership and management, including numerous myths, illusions, folklore, and superstitions [12, 13].

Thus far we have examined the role of preconception in guiding leaders' thinking and actions and how difficult situations arise. Continued commitment to ancient and now-archaic preconceptions invite all kinds of problems – from big ones that threaten brand, reputation, or company existence to the myriad small problems of day-to-day operations – that leaders hate to be bothered with. These difficulties, invariably misattributed as "people problems," are not preordained, nor must they be seen as irritating. We have preconceptions about problems that, if changed, can lead to improved situations with greater stability as shown in Figure 2-3 (Pyramid of Rationalities). Leaders do not have to be prisoners of their preconceptions. The next chapter will examine how difficult situations can be made less common and less difficult to reduce human stress and frustration and enable greater human flourishing on a resource constrained planet.

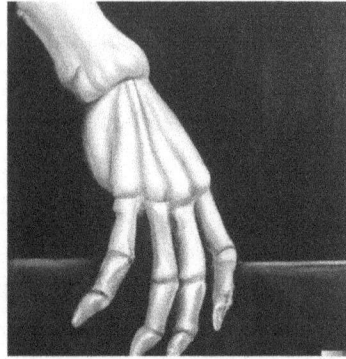

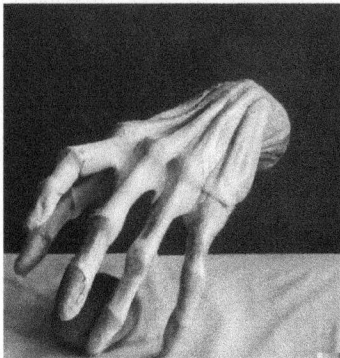

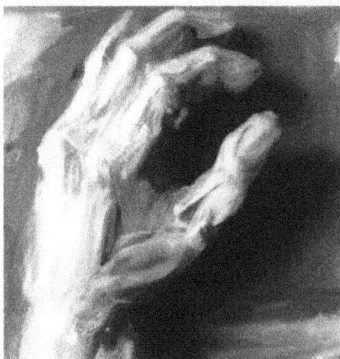

Figure 2-4. AI generated (DALL·E 2) images depicting the dead hand of the past, still guiding the present.

THINK

- Referring to Figure 2-1, which threat do top leaders see as being the greatest: efficiency, process improvement, creativity, or social change? Explain why.

- Referring to Figure 2-2, can you pinpoint times at work where information feedback changed one or more of the preconceptions listed in Chapter 1. How so?

THINK

- Referring to Figure 2-2, can you pinpoint experiences at work that changed one or more of the preconceptions listed in Chapter 1. How so?

- Referring to the lists of preconceptions Chapter 1 and Figure 2-3, which preconceptions are the most destabilizing? Explain why.

THINK

- What preconceptions do you have about problems?

- When leaders attribute problems to people (i.e., anthropomorphize problems), which preconceptions listed in Chapter 1 are they connecting to?

Notes

[1] I refer to this type of leadership as that which is associated with "classical management;" colloquially, "the old way of thinking and doing things" or "traditional way of thinking and doing things." It embodies an "originalist" sentiment wherein the original ways of leading and managing people are seen as good and right, then as now (with some forced modifications), and carries with it an appearance of objectivity and thus a high value. In contrast, progressive forms of management such as 1910s Scientific Management, 1970s Toyota Management, and 1980s Lean management, the latter two of which are in current practice, embrace a humanist philosophy – a philosophy of leadership and management without theism, though not totally devoid of supernatural preconceptions. As a humanist way to comprehend leadership and management, it acknowledges causality and people's purposive role in human affairs. It rests on a different set of preconceptions, a different metaphysics, learned mostly through the process of kaizen. As such, there is a conscious, rather than unconscious, commitment to many metaphysical elements.

[2] I say "appears" because climate change or other significant short- or long-term event will likely derail the meliorative trend – if it exists at all.

[3] The late-2022 "return to office" demanded by many top leaders.

[4] Porter, M. (1979), "How Competitive Forces Shape

Strategy," *Harvard Business Review*, Volume 57, Number 2, May, pp. 137–145

[5] Both Porter's framework and Figure 2-1 accept the preconceptions presented in Chapter 1 as the starting point of inquiry. That is, power, conquest, and dominance over collaboration, teamwork, and mutually beneficial outcomes – despite most leaders' words to the contrary.

[6] Argyris, C. and Schön, D. (1974). *Theory in Practice. Increasing Professional Effectiveness*, Jossey-Bass, San Francisco, California

[7] These modifications to the Argyris and Schön's single- and double-loop learning models were developed by Emiliani in August 2022.

[8] Figure 2-2a and 2-2b make no claim as to the correctness of decision-making. It is only to show how learning succeeds or fails; how mental models change or not, and how progress is or is not made.

[9] Kirsch, A. (2022), "The People Cheering for Humanity's End: A Disparate Group of Thinkers Says We Should Welcome Our Demise," *The Atlantic*, January/February 2023, https://www.theatlantic.com/magazine/archive/2023/01/anthropocene-anti-humanism-transhumanism-apocalypse-predictions/672230/, accessed 1 December 2022

[10] Double-loop learning is brilliant and indispensable, not just for CEOs, for human survival, improving the human

habitat, and human experience, but for solving any type of problem better and more quickly by anyone at any level in the organization. It also helps negate the traditional cost-benefit analysis that precedes decision-making because such analyses are based on archaic preconceptions. Cost-benefit analysis approaches irrelevancy when survival is as stake.

[11] Likewise, traditions, myths, superstitions, and legends are made to be normal or natural, and thus acceptable to impede progress or make the status quo seem desirable. They include knowledge that cannot be verified by experience, and thus diminish human agency. It is a cultural conditioning that justifies the common sense of the community.

[12] A right and privilege of leaders is to make decision based on whatever information they judge relevant, ranging from facts to myths, illusions, folklore, and superstitions to personal predilections, and any combination thereof. All human information processing and decision-making contains real or potential defects. The relevant task as a leader is to improve their thinking and decision-making using as much high-fidelity information as possible while minimizing low-fidelity information (e.g., archaic preconceptions, myths, illusions, folklore, superstitions, etc.).

[13] The famous Beer Game, which simulates the dynamics of supply chain, is supposed to teach participants about the bullwhip effect and how to avoid it. Yet, numerous preconceptions remain in place that result in continuing occurrences of the bullwhip effect. See https://en.wikipedia.org/wiki/Bullwhi p_effect.

3

Difficult Situations

What is readily apparent in hierarchical organization is the widely accepted preconception that problems are bad and that there exists a repetition of problems. The same types of problems pop up over and over again. These problems are common among organizations and span different industries. While each organization seems unique, people who have worked in different companies or industries realize that uniqueness is largely an illusion when it comes to problems. The problems may have different names and involve different products or services, but they share a common ground of poor human information processing [1]. This is due to non-use or poor use of structured problem-solving processes and the overriding influence of social problem-solving processes. Structured problem-solving is informed primarily by facts, logic, and truth. Social problem-solving processes are informed by these as well as:

- Status
- Traditions
- Myths
- Aesthetics
- Subjective standards of value or worth
- Benefits and losses
- Biases and stereotypes

These subjective social influences, combined with the

"problems are bad" preconception, contaminate problem-solving (*absence of reason*) such that root causes are difficult or impolitic to identify and correct. Consequently, problems fester and grow larger, and some erupt into major business problems that command top leaders' attention. These types of problems are generally time-consuming for leaders and costly for the company. Top leaders, being profoundly sensitive to criticism and enjoying the status and deference accorded by others, have unusual success at blaming their difficulties on other people, organizations, or things. Nevertheless, the damage is done, and leaders pay the reputational price and the subsequent costs incurred in litigation and to rebuild the brand. Is this destiny or choice?

As leaders ascend hierarchies, they become more distant from the day-to-day problems that occur at lower levels of the organization. Given their free ability to choose, most leaders prefer to spend their time in conference rooms deliberating the larger problems associated with money-making and stock price appreciation: strategy, sales growth, market share, deal-making to blunt or eliminate competitive threats, soirees, and the like. They ensconce themselves in the metaphysical world by choice [2], and in doing so negate the real world where problems incubate and slowly grow (see Figure 2-2b, top).

This detachment from the real world means leaders can have only an abstract understanding of work processes. Any understanding of work processes they possess was formed decades earlier and is surely antiquated. Problems that arise with the expectation that they will be put to rest by lower-level managers working in a (typically) blame-oriented environment greatly incentivizes them to ignore or cover up problems, thus obscuring or rejecting cumulative causal sequence. Therefore, leaders, whether they realize it or not, take on a supernatural, fatalistic view of problem occurrence. Theirs is a deductive stance of "There is a problem, go fix it," rather than an inductive stance of "What problems can occur and how should we avoid them?" So, like hot flowing to cold (i.e., the second law of thermodynamics), problems come to leaders as opposed to leaders coming to problems. The only question is the types of problems and their severity, followed by what actions to take, recognizing that our adaptive abilities will be constrained by the preconceptions listed in Chapter 1. This forms the grounds for repetitive problems (Figure 2-3, pyramid of irrationalities), and causes people to labor far beyond that which is necessary. Yet, because people are being paid by the company (often intimately personalized as being paid directly by the top leader), leaders' preconception is that they have the right to waste people's time and thus their lives (and many other resources) for that which leaders have consciously chosen to be inattentive to.

In a world where processes permeate all aspect of life, it is an untenable position for leaders to claim that they, either individually or as an Institution of leadership, can be separate from it – an immutable object in an intrinsically dynamic environment of continuous change. Under such circumstances, there is little reflective thinking during and after action. Unchanging habits prevail, rather than modification of habits according to circumstances. Fresh thinking about leadership and fresh practice are destined to be both rare and short-lived, as is empirically observed. The result is a general lowering of intelligence with respect to problem recognition and problem-solving. Also consider artificial intelligence systems, soon to be offering "expert" advice to top leaders, are developed by humans and learn from humans, and, increasingly, itself, contain most or all the preconceptions listed in Chapter 1. AI may encumber leaders with the same types of difficult problems – the one's that consume a lot of leadership and organizational resources for protracted periods of time – that leaders have long experienced. What types of problems are these and in what ways can they be corrected? More than problem-solving, how can difficult problems be recognized early in their growth process and prevented from germinating?

The tables on the following three pages provide evidence of the sowing, germination, and growth process of problems in organizations. The metric in use and associated beliefs as to its favorability are rooted in the following preconceptions which are taken by leaders to be fact (culled from Chapter 1):

Whatever is, is right	Outsourcing lowers costs
Respect traditions	Ignore Feedback
Hierarchical control	One Best Way
Self-Interest	Infallibility
Growth	Linear Thinking
Manage with measures	Need doers, not thinkers

The contents of the tables reflect the results of questions posed to full-time employees with years of work experience [3]. As such, their answers reflect real-world conditions in a wide variety of service and manufacturing organizations.

Metric in Use	Leadership Belief (favorable)	Worker Behavior (unfavorable)	Worker Competency (unfavorable)
Projects completed on time	On time is good, late is bad	Deliver on time, quality often bad	Disregard for quality
Projects competed on budget	On budget is good, under budget is not good, over budget is very bad	Padding of estimates	Never learn how to estimate properly; learn how to pad
Cost of quality	Small number is good quality	Hide quality problems	Game the metric
First call resolution	Resolving client problem quickly means greater customer satisfaction	Resolve ticket on first call even if there is additional work that should be done	Providing reduced service
Total tickets logged	More calls logged tech support is working hard and doing good work	Techs log calls for anything and everything to boost total tickets logged	Logging unnecessary calls
Compliance to standard bidding process	Compliance yields good results	Don't deviate from process	Don't improve the process
Labor absorption	Must maximize labor absorption	Produce units requiring more labor	Increase inventories
Customer satisfaction survey results	Results prove the organization is customer-focused	Pressure clients to complete the survey and give excellent rating, or don't tell client about survey to avoid negative rating	Game the system and introduce bias in survey results
Number of escapes	Quality problems must not reach the marketplace	Increase number of inspections	Increase costs and lead-time
Weekly status reports	Track what employees are working on	Scramble to assemble weekly status report	Reports focused on quantity of input vs. quality

Metric in Use	Leadership Belief (favorable)	Worker Behavior (unfavorable)	Worker Competency (unfavorable)
Percent monthly production (actual vs. scheduled)	>95% there is no problem, <95% means overtime is required	Do minimum work necessary to meet quotas	Game system to get overtime pay
Equipment uptime	Equipment downtime is bad	Keep equipment running	Run equipment until failure
Patients per hour	More patients per hours yield higher revenue and profits	Spend less time with patients	Reduce quality of care
Percent engineering changes completed	High percent is favorable	Focus on completing the ECs vs. assuring change made properly	Ignore data trends or larger configuration system problems
Perform average of six corrections per hour	All errors are the same	Focus on correcting easiest errors	Avoid difficult errors
Customer satisfaction survey results	Survey results prove company is customer-focused	Pressure clients to give excellent rating or don't tell client about survey to avoid negative rating	Game system and introduce bias in survey results
Forecast accuracy	Software/human predictions are accurate	Constantly adjust metric to make the numbers	Focus on internal metric vs. actual customer needs
Outsourcing	Outsourcing lowers costs	Outsource anything that gets you to the number faster	Fix the work produced by outsourcing company
Sales	Current year sales must exceed previous year sales	Pressure customers to purchase more products; upsell	Indifferent to actual customer needs
Sales per employee	Represents productivity and effective use of resources.	Increase sales by any means	Selling things to customers that they do not need
Total lost time injuries	Injuries cost money	Pressure to not report injuries	Workers hide injuries

Metric in Use	Leadership Belief (favorable)	Worker Behavior (unfavorable)	Worker Competency (unfavorable)
Number of lines of code per day	Indicates skill levels of software developers (more = better)	Focus on quantity of code vs. quality of code	Write more lines of code than is necessary
Number of sales calls to doctors' offices per day	More calls will increase sales.	Visit doctors even if you know they won't buy	Don't understand doctor's needs
Variance to budget	Drives discipline to meeting budget	Play budget games to avoid unfavorable variances	Ignore opportunities to improve process
Enrollment	Year-over-year increases in enrollments is good	Find new students; create new programs	Lower standards for admission; re-package existing programs
Graduation rate	High graduation rate means school is doing a good work	Make it easier for students to pass courses	Be less demanding of self and of students
Complete X training modules by Y (date)	Employees will perform better with training	Complete training modules on-time	Compliance, not learning
Percent network uptime	True measure of network performance	Report less than actual number of downtime events	Maintain current environment vs. improve services
Average time to resolve Help desk tickets	Response time misses motivate improved performance	Take only the easy tickets	Focus on numbers vs. client satisfaction
Number of code changes per month	Number of changes indicates value of employee	Grab easy changes; make single change into multiple changes	Gaming the system
Meeting attendance	Attendance reflects engagement and participation	Show up; check-the-box	Attending

It is evident that the workers' behaviors and competencies are not what leaders have in mind when they speak of "flawless execution," "failure is not an option," or "teamwork." Yet leaders are inattentive and thus unaware of the unfavorable behaviors and unfavorable competencies that their metrics develop in employees due to their self-imposed distance from the real world of employees' work. Remarkably, some leaders who rise within the function, such as from purchasing agent (buyer) to vice president of purchasing (supply chain), are fully aware of the unfavorable behaviors and unfavorable competencies produced by metrics such as purchase price variance, but they continue to favor the use of the metric. In this way, an officer of the company sets the company up for unwanted problems. But he or she is not alone. The leadership team in its entirety knowing or unknowingly perform their duties starting on a foundation of preconceptions that will surely cause recurring problems and costly crises.

Each metric listed in the tables function as leaders' "plan" for performance, while the "actual" is what the employees do day-to-day. Leaders, of course, own the metric and are certain to face ever-larger problems because they are unaware of the gap between plan and actual. Preconceptions thus sow a process whereby problems germinate and grow into larger problems. Leaders, unaware of the root of the problem immediately invoke the preconception that people are the problem. They take no responsibility at all and blame the workers. In this way we can easily see how leaders' preconceptions inform simplistic ways of thinking befitting their status, but which cause them the problems, varied in type and magnitude, that they hope to avoid. Employees, for their part, are loath to tell leaders their secrets of survival in a dysfunctional environment for fear of blame and retribution. The instrumental relationship that leaders have with employees, rooted in social and economic preconceptions, makes business anything but efficient.

Leaders mistakenly assume metrics that have been in use for a long time, or the metrics found in turnkey software systems, have been vetted long ago and are good and right to use. That bad assumption illustrates an unwillingness to question things and instead subscribe to the Foundational Preconception "whatever is, is right." An obvious solution is to work with employees, not consultants [4], to identify or create metrics that eliminate unfavorable behaviors and unfavorable competencies. This requires leaders to disengage from their metaphysical world and enter the real world to understand the effect that performance metrics have on employees and other stakeholders such as suppliers. Such disengagement must happen regularly (see Figure 2-2b, bottom image) or risk the germination and growth of self-inflicted problems.

The problems leaders face are many and varied, and require them to evaluate information inputs and make decisions. However, awareness of the nature of the problem is limited by the available information, which is often incomplete, sporadic, and distorted given the difficulty of upward information flow in hierarchies and organizational politics [5]. Consequently, it is difficult for leaders to make sense of problems and determine their severity, which in turn affects the quality and timeliness of decision-making and types and numbers of subsequent actions taken to correct the problem. The result is ineffective problem solving, the likely recurrence of problems, and the sowing, germination, and growth of new (or related) problems.

Deficiencies in sense-making can be corrected using the Cynefin® (pronounced *kuh-nev-in*) framework [6], Figure 3-1. Cynefin is a conceptual sense-making framework for leaders used to establish context in support of decision-making, where sense-making means "making sense of the world in order to act in it" [6, p. 15]. This dynamic framework depicts problem-spaces that help improve sense-making by

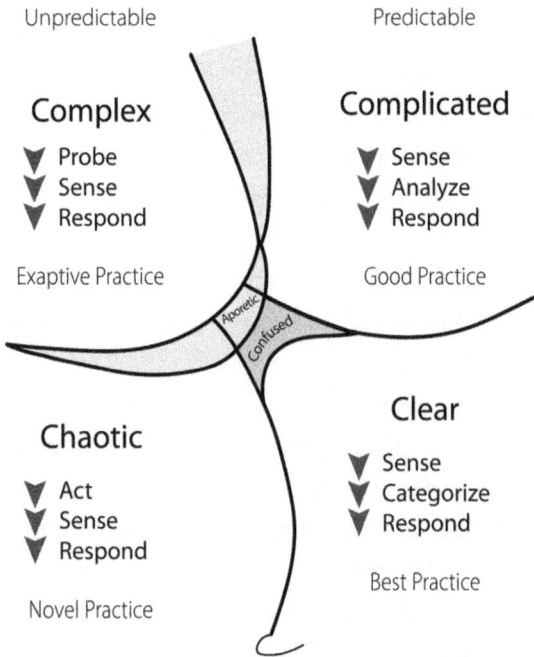

Figure 3-1. Cynefin® framework for decision-making [6].

understanding the three primary systems and liminal zones (transition states between domains): order, complexity, and chaos in the context of enabling and limiting constraints. The framework describes five domains: Clear and Complicated (ordered, predictable), Complex and Chaotic (unpredictable), and Aporetic/Confused [7]. Sense-making is a knowledge generating activity that develops a common understanding of a problem leading to improved decision-making. Readers are referred to Note 5 for authoritative descriptions of the Cynefin framework and examples of its use.

While the Cynefin framework challenges beliefs and best practices, it uncritically accepts preconceptions, invariably those cited in Chapter 1, as the starting point of inquiry: i.e., "Cynefin is about how things are, how we know them and how we perceive them" [6, p. 45] and "adjacent possibles" [6, p. 67]. So, one could say the outlook of Cynefin regarding preconceptions is "whatever is, is right," and it is this outlook that forms the basis for sense-making and subsequent decision-making. That means there is a high probability that new decisions will be consistent with past decisions, according to the maxim [8]:

"What's next is most likely to be determined by what *is*."

In terms of causality, we can think of Clear as one-dimensional (linear) cause-and-effect, Complicated as two-dimensional (planar) causes-and-effect (e.g., Ishikawa diagram), Complex as three-dimensional causes-and-effect (volume; Ishikawa diagram with z-axis rib connections), and Chaos as n-dimensional (indeterminate) causes-and-effects.

Thus, problem-solving would proceed from basic methods to more advanced structured methods to trial and error to random testing. The domains Clear and Complicated are ordered and thus outcome of change is predictable. Complex and Chaotic (random) are unordered and unpredictable. This makes outcomes of change unpredictable due to entanglement of people, organizations, processes, etc.

The Cynefin framework is useful as a typology for getting people onto a structured path for making sense of the situation they face [9]. It is a both a prelude to problem-solving and direction for problem-solving and subsequent decision-making. However, classical management, the traditional way of leading and managing organizations [10], is rooted in preconceptions about how best to acquire and process information. Sense-making is based on information provided to leaders by subordinates – conference room sense-making – rather than leaders engaging their senses of touch, sight, hearing, smell, and taste by experiencing the problem first-hand. In other words, the world of the executive is far different than the world of the hands-on worker. These different contexts produce different sense-making outcomes and subsequent decision-making.

For example, the sense-making of workers led to the early recognition of complex problems with Boeing's 737 Max aircraft that were not acknowledged in top leader's sense-making. The result was a series of poor decision-making by top leaders both before and after the two airplane crashes. Boeing leaders' sense-making operated under the illusion that problems existed in the Clear or Complicated domains [11].

This is typical of how leaders see things, the result of overconfidence in their analytical capabilities and unwillingness to bend to inconvenient realities. Preconceptions are the strong and resilient scaffolding that supports the status quo (Figure 3-2). The scaffolding is an interconnected network of more than 150 economic, social, political, historical, philosophical, spiritual, aesthetic, technological, and legal preconceptions. It is overdesigned such that changing or removing a few preconceptions (horizontal or vertical tubes) does not affect the overall integrity of the network of preconceptions that form the Institution of Leadership and System of Profound Privilege. That is why efforts to improve leadership by changing leadership behaviors have had little success.

Figure 3-2. AI generated (DALL·E 2) image depicting scaffolding, a metaphor for the strength of the status quo due to the interconnectedness of economic, social, political, historical, philosophical, spiritual, aesthetic, technological, and legal preconceptions.

The scaffold of preconceptions – built over centuries, highly regarded by most leaders, and nearly permanent in its existence – supports tradition and prohibits them from engaging human sensory perceptions in the process of sense-making. Sensory perceptions are critically important for breaking the status quo, which may or may not be an objective of a team that uses the Cynefin framework. They may instead use it as a guide to find the right solution for different sets of conditions informed by the existing scaffold of preconceptions.

Leaders' preconceptions, rooted in classical management, form a knowledge-reality universe that they use to recognize problems, analyze problems, and make decisions. We will call this Knowledge-Reality Universe I (KRU-I). Using KRU-I, leaders are likely to find themselves in one difficult situation after another (Complex and Chaotic domains). KRU-I will again be used to correct the problems that produced the difficult situation, likely prolonging resolution and producing future difficult situations. These difficult situations are unpleasant and costly in different ways.

Given the ubiquity of newsworthy corporate problems ranging from products that injure or kill customers, services that disappoint customers, bankruptcies, disputes with suppliers, employee unionization and strikes, fraud, and shareholder lawsuits, we can confidently say that the constellation of preconceptions that leaders have are not the constellation of preconceptions that leaders need to solve problems well (Figure 3-3). What does "solve problems well" mean? It means to solve problems such that their recurrence is eliminated, or the probability of their recurrence is significantly reduced, including a reduction of negative externalities (e.g., improve human health in the workplace, protect the natural environment). The gap between KRU-I (spiritual, teleological) and KRU-II (material, fact) is wide and not easily spanned, as evidenced by the ready acceptance of classical management across generations of leaders.

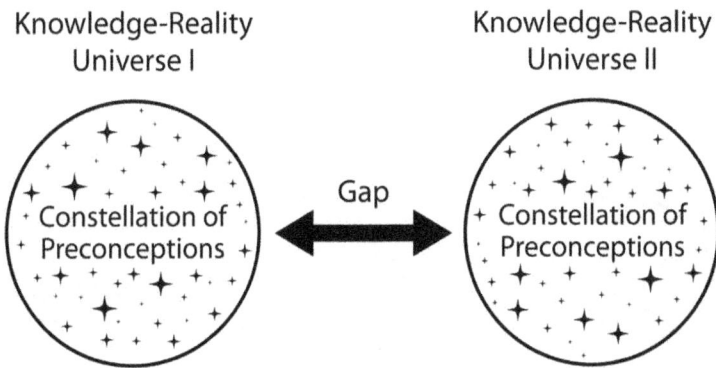

Figure 3-3. Gap between the preconceptions leaders have versus the preconceptions leaders need to solve a problem well.

Moving from KRU-I to KRU-II is very difficult because it involves thinking in ways and doing things that are prohibited by the Institution of Leadership and System of Profound Privilege, e.g., experiencing problems first-hand as workers do versus having an abstract or idealized understanding of the problem that comes from conference room sense-making. It is "unnatural," and thus a major cultural challenge.

One can think of the constellation of KRU-I preconceptions as being the larger habitat in which the Cynefin framework resides. This "business as usual" scaffold forms the basis for sense-making and analysis of a problem that then leads to decisions (Figure 3-4). The Foundational Preconception, "whatever is, is right," describes KRU-I [12]. Starting with a different constellation of preconceptions, KRU-II, forms a different basis for sense-making and analysis of a problem that then leads to different decisions. Its Foundational Preconception is "whatever is, is wrong." Consequently, one would expect sense-making and subsequent decision-making to be substantially different for nearly every problem encountered.

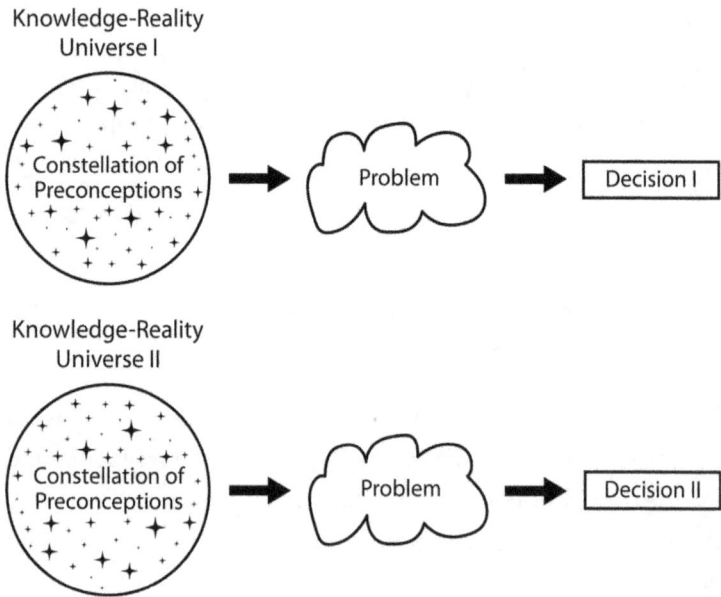

Figure 3-4. Constellation of preconceptions lead to interpreting problems in different ways on the path towards making a decision.

KRU-II is a changed perspective compared to KRU-I, more reality-based than metaphysically-based. Running an organization by the numbers and making data-driven decisions sow the seeds of varied problems that will germinate and grow. Numbers are an illusion of reality, not reality itself [13]. There is the reality of shop and office floor work, and then there is the metaphysics of running the business. Leaders make elaborate investments to transform physical reality into electronic metaphysical representations using computer systems (Figure 3-5). Workers' reality (R) is transformed (T) into metaphysical (M) numbers for analysis and decision-making (D) by leaders. Leaders believe M equals R, but M is always less than R because it is devoid of human senses. This introduces errors in leaders' decision-making,

Workers' Material Reality
Based on Sensory Perception
Truth • Know-How

Leaders' Metaphysical Reality
External to Sense Perception
Interpret Numbers • Make Decisions

Figure 3-5. Transforming (T) workers' reality into metaphysical information (numbers) for leadership decision-making (D).

oftentimes negatively impacting workers' and other stakeholders, and sometimes leaders themselves. Several of the Foundational Preconceptions listed in Chapter 1 form the basis for leaders' belief that M equals R.

Let's illustrate the point about the transformation of workers' reality to leaders' metaphysics with two concrete examples. Here is the first example [14]:

> "An example familiar to everyone is meteorology. The layman observes the weather directly through his senses. He sees blue sky, clouds, snow, and lightning; he hears thunder; he feels wind, temperature and humidity; at times he tastes a fog and smells storms. The meteorologist can make these direct observations as well as a layman; but instead of relying upon his sense impressions he uses a battery of recording instruments — thermographs, barographs, anemometers, wind vanes, psychrometers, hygrographs, precipitation gauges, sunshine recorders, and so on. That is, he transforms much that he can sense, and some things that he cannot sense, into numerous sets of symbols stripped of all the vivid qualities of personal experience. It is with these symbols from his own station and with similar symbols sent to him by other observers dotted over continents and oceans that he works. They show the weather broken down into numerous factors, which he must put together again in his mind. To that end he plots certain of his symbols on a weather map, which he compares with

maps drawn a few hours earlier. From these maps, a new set of symbols, he derives conclusions about air masses of different types and about the weather likely to be produced by their movements and internal changes. By these highly artificial operations, he arrives at forecasts concerning actual conditions over wide areas, that will soon be judged right or wrong by millions who sense their local weather."

In this example, we see that ultimate arbiter of truth is not the meteorologist, but the people who experience weather. In the context of business, the ultimate arbiter of truth is the worker, not the top leader. Unfortunately, the Institution of Leadership and System of Profound Privilege unconditionally disallows workers from being the ultimate arbiter of truth. Here is the second example [15]:

"For the intermittent process of making steel in a furnace with its heat and noise, its dim shadows and blinding glares, they substitute a column of figures purporting to show how many tons of steel ingots have been turned out by all the furnaces in a given area during successive days or weeks. That colorless record gives no faintest idea of what the operation looks like or feels like; it does not tell whether the work is hard or easy, well or ill paid, profitable or done at a loss. It suggests continuous operation, which is achieved at no furnace. It hides differences of location and types of product. And it separates the one act of turning out tonnage from all the other activities with which it is interwoven. Many, though not all, of these interrelated changes are likewise recorded in columns of figures; but each record is as devoid of reality and as divorced from its matrix as the record of tons produced... Then he must mix a large element of personal judgment into his comparisons. In trying to compose a picture... from these diverse materials, the would-be objective student is forced to devise further artifices... We are, in truth, transmuting actual experience in the workaday world into something new and strange, much as a meteorologist transforms our experience of sunshine into new and strange symbols that record solar radiation. The hazards of our undertaking are many."

Indeed, there are great hazards in undertaking the transformation from reality to the metaphysics that leaders find palatable. KRU-I is instrumental to leaders' reality. Yet, many leaders have suffered or been felled by KRU-I preconceptions. Despite that, one generation of leaders after the next embraces KRU-I. Whatever is, is right, no matter how wrong it may be.

To a significant extent, leaders have a choice of the types of problems they must deal with. A continuous barrage of problems in the Complex and Chaotic domains, mistakenly thought to be in Clear and Complicated domains due to status, is not appealing. Yet the status quo tends to prevail, giving continued life to KRU-I preconceptions (see Figure 2-2b, top). In contrast, KRU-II leaders generally find themselves in fewer and less severe difficult situations. These would be the leaders who engage the real world as shown in Figure 2-2b (bottom image), which helps prevent germination and growth of many types of problems [16].

KRU-I is not the end or final term of leadership. Something comes after that, and again after that, etc., in an evolutionary process of adapting to changing social and technological conditions. This leads to the question, what is the process for changing preconceptions? It could occur in different deliberative (fast) and nondeliberative (slow) ways:

- A book you read
- Persuasion by a peer
- Engaging worker's real world through your own initiative or hands-on training workshops
- Assistance from an app
- Unknown emergent methods
- Evolution itself

Perhaps all the above. Leaders who migrate from KRU-I to KRU-II will no doubt face strong peer pressure to remain with the KRU-I in-group, perhaps enticed by more money or greater responsibility. Emerging leaders must navigate that terrain as best they can. It will not be easy and could cost them their job. But one thing is apparent; archaic preconceptions need to be laid to rest and replaced with preconceptions that are right for the times and that have greater emphasis on humanism and on the well-being of future generations.

THINK

- Identify other examples:

Metric in Use	Leadership Belief (favorable)	Worker Behavior (unfavorable)	Worker Competency (unfavorable)

THINK

- Looking at the preconceptions listed in Chapter 1, which Foundational, Economic, Social, Political, and Historical preconceptions for KRU-I would change or be eliminated to form KRU-II (a changed perspective)?

THINK

- Identify philosophical, spiritual, aesthetic, technological, and legal preconceptions associated with KRU-I. These would be aligned with the preconceptions listed in Chapter 1.

THINK

- Identify philosophical, spiritual, aesthetic, technological, and legal preconceptions associated with KRU-II.

THINK

- Regarding Figure 3-5, which preconceptions listed in Chapter 1 make leaders think that M = R (metaphysical representations are equivalent to reality)?

Notes

[1] For a practical exposition of defects in leadership information processing, see Emiliani, B. and Torinesi, M. (2021), *Wheel of Fortune: Getting to the Heart of Business Strategy*, Cubic LLC, South Kingstown, Rhode Island

[2] Top leaders' metaphysical world comprises both their work (e.g., money-making) and the preconceptions listed in Chapter 1.

[3] The origin of this information is from a homework assignment given to graduate students in course titled "Innovative Leadership." The students were full-time working professionals with an average of about 10 years of work experience. The assignment was: "List 3 to 5 metrics used in your department to track performance. Identify the favorable beliefs that must exist in the mind of senior management in order to support the use of these metrics. What are the resulting unfavorable behaviors and unfavorable competencies among the workers who are held accountable to the metrics?"

[4] Employees have the intelligence necessary to help develop metrics that promote favorable behaviors, competencies, and business results. This can be used as an opportunity for collaboration, relationship-building, trust-building, and mutually beneficial outcomes.

[5] Like hypertension, blocked information flows are the "silent killers" of companies.

[6] Snowden, D. and Friends (2022), *Cynefin: Weaving Sense-Making into the Fabric of Our World*, Second Edition, Cognitive Edge Ltd., The Cynefin Company. Cynefin® is a registered trademark of Cognitive Edge Ltd. Cynefin means "habitat" in Welsh. See also https://cynefin.io/wiki/Main_Page

[7] Definitions: "Exaptive: The taking of an idea, concept, tool, method, framework, etc., intended to address one thing, and using it to address a different thing, often in another domain." "Novel: Different from anything known or existing before, possibly resulting from exaptation." "Aporetic: …the epistemological state of not having made sense of a given context, while being aware of such ignorance and having an intentional attitude towards overcoming it. Also, the liminal portion of the 'confused' domain." "Confused: …a state of not knowing the type of decision domain being faced, while not necessarily being aware of that." Source: https://cynefin .io/wiki/Glossary, accessed 12 December 2022

[8] Dowd, D. (1958), *Thorstein Veblen*, Cornell University Press, Ithaca, New York, p. 157

[9] Snowden, D. and Boone, M. (2007), "A Leader's Framework for Decision-Making," *Harvard Business Review*, Volume 85, November, pp. 69-76

[10] Emiliani, B. (2018), *The Triumph of Classical Management Over Lean Management: How Tradition Prevails and What to Do About It*, Cubic LLC, South Kingstown, Rhode Island

[11] Boeing leaders, physically and mentally far removed

from the reality of the factory, run the business from the metaverse of corporate headquarters informed by KRU-I preconceptions. Boeing leadership is not unique in this regard. This disconnection from reality, is a feature, not a bug, of the Institution of Leadership and System of Profound Privilege and has long been common in business and other types of organizations. Consequently, worker efficiency and productivity are perpetually limited by the constraints of inefficiency imposed onto workers by leaders.

[12] The preconception "whatever is, is right" places extraordinary and unwarranted faith in the ability of humans to expertly make sense of the systems they reside in, the problems that emerge from it, and the ability to solve problems without errors. As such, it doubles as a spiritual preconception. The Cynefin framework eloquently proves that faith to be misplaced.

[13] There are times when numbers can accurately reflect reality, but leaders may ignore that information if it is inconvenient to their interests. It is their right and privilege to do so, but it may not be without consequences; e.g. data shows that remote work due to COVID-19 is a success, yet many leaders want workers to return to the office. The resultant worker unhappiness will likely manifest itself in lower engagement and reduced productivity. Source: "It's Time to Reimagine Where and How Work Will Get Done," (2021), PwC, https://www.pwc.com/us/en/services/consul ting/business-transformation/library/covid-19-us-remote-w ork-survey.html, 12 January, accessed 19 December 2022

[14] Burns, A.F. and Mitchell, W.C. (1946), *Measuring Business Cycles: Studies in Business Cycles No. 2*, National Bureau of Economic Research, New York, New York, pp. 14-15

[15] Ibid., pp. 15-17

[16] In the same way that beliefs are not uniformly the same among people and how single- and-double-loop learning differ between leaders and workers, Cynefin likewise differs. KRU-I (Institution of Leadership and System of Profound Privilege compared to KRU-II (Institution of Workmanship and System of Profound Knowledge) have their own preconceptual basis for making sense of problems in each of the domains (Figure 3-6). While Cynefin is applicable to both universes, there are large differences in the understanding of problems (and who is impacted by problems), as well as different problem-solving methods and decisions.

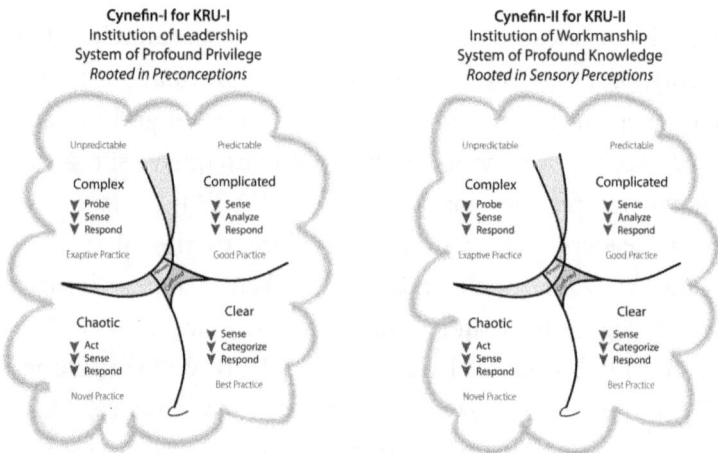

Figure 3-6. Preconceptual basis for making sense of problems varies according to the social habits of thought and action characteristic of KRU-I and KRU-II.

4

Changing Your Perspective

Where do we go from here? I do not live in your shoes. I do not know your experiences, your aspirations, your joys, or your sorrows. I do not know your life, your job, or the work-related challenges that you face every day. Therefore, I cannot say what the next steps are for you as an individual or for leaders as a group. You must find your own way.

You have serious work to do. In the subsequent pages, please write the final chapter. Write a narrative or outline your thoughts in bullet form. Get started in the direction of implementation; how to become a better leader than those before you. Use a pencil so that you can make corrections. Take the information that I have provided and use your intelligence and write your own unique ending to this book. Reflect and think before your write. Has your perspective changed? How so, and what does it mean for your leadership?

Consider the following: How will you use what I have written to elucidate the changes you need to make to be a better leader, a more responsible leader, one who is more mindful of negative externalities, and who elevates their sense-making, problem-solving, and decision-making capabilities? How do you avoid being stuck in the past? How will you more fully engage curiosity? What preconceptions stand in the way? What preconceptions should be left behind? What new preconceptions do you need to gain, and how will you do that? What is the process?

What must you learn, study, or discover? Who should you call upon if you need help? As an emerging (or established) leader, what future do you want to create? Do you want your leadership to evolve? Why? How? What would be new and better? How will you do it? You will not do it alone, so what kind of help will you need from colleagues and those who report to you? How will you gain followers, most of whom are knowingly or unknowingly aligned with the preconceptions listed in Chapter 1?

Leading better is not enough. How will you continuously teach and train the next generation of leaders? What will they need to learn and practice? How will that change over time? What process helps ensure training is in-step with individual and organizational needs? How will customers or other stakeholders inform the choices that are made? You may someday achieve your vision of the future through close collaboration with many people. What comes next? How will you know when preconceptions that were once new cross a boundary and become outdated? How will you know when traditions are no longer useful? Or there may be traditions, long outdated, that need to come back into use to help make needed progress. How will you know?

I have given you much to think about. One thing is clear: you do not have all the answers, and you never will. Recognizing this, you do not need to touch upon each point made or each question raised in the preceding paragraphs. Just get started writing your creative journey towards a changed perspective and be prepared to revisit and revise and improve it often as time passes. Be my co-author. The next nine pages are yours.

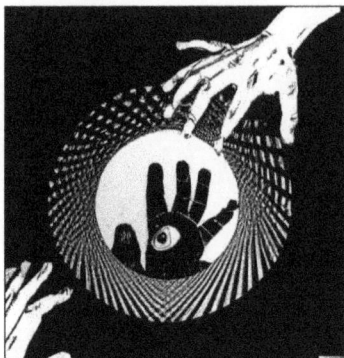

Figure 4-1. AI generated (DALL·E 2) images depicting a changed perspective.

Closing Comments

The purpose of this book is to challenge the settled view that better leadership is brought about simply by changing leaders' behaviors. Having made four categories of preconceptions explicit as objects for analysis, it becomes clear that by starting with beliefs,

Beliefs → Behaviors → Competencies

one is forced to accept the preconceptions listed in Chapter 1, *formed prior to experience* and in the *absence of reasoning*, as static and unchangeable [1]. Preconceptions are difficult to change, but they are not static. They can change over time and experiences can be had such they revise or eliminate archaic or irrelevant preconceptions. Thus, the applicable construct is:

Preconceptions → Beliefs → Behaviors → Competencies

The implications for education, training, and development are profound [2]. Efforts to solve difficult problems can begin with an explication of preconceptions specific to the context of the problem as well as the preconceptions that surround and support the problem's existence (scaffolding). This changes the initial approach to problem-solving. It also changes the approach to analyzing failures by identifying the preconceptions that contributed to failure and subsequent revision or elimination of those preconceptions to prevent future failures. This is especially relevant in the leadership and management of business, where failure can be traced to the preconceptions listed in Chapter 1 [3].

In the contexts of sense-making and problem-solving, it suggests a revision to the question, "What if our thinking about this is all wrong?" An improvement would be the statement, "Our thinking about this is probably wrong." For that you can use the Cynefin framework, but be sure to take it a step further to make your preconceptions explicit and question each one. As economist Wesley C. Mitchell said [4]:

> "...we should not be the dupes of our preconceptions. We have them, whether we like it or not. Best to work them as explicitly as we can. Must make sure that details are logically consistent with them. But it is naive to fancy that what is common sense to us will appeal as common sense to later generations. This is the most dazzlingly disconcerting of Veblen's insights-the hardest to live with, but also the most enlightening."

It has long been the habit of humans to ignore, deny, or discard the metaphysical foundation of our thinking, our problems, and our problem-solving in any organizational setting. In doing so we oftentimes have more the illusion of progress than actual progress, as one generation after the next repeats the same mistakes – albeit in a different time and place. Extant superficiality opens the door to further inquiry of phenomena that beg for better understanding to produce better outcomes; i.e.,

- The role of preconception in guiding leaders' thinking and actions, as well as follower's ready uptake of leaders' preconceptions
- How difficult situations arise and why difficult situations are accepted as a *fait accompli*
- How can difficult situations be made less common and less difficult to reduce human stress and frustration and enable greater human flourishing on a resource constrained planet

Humans have the ability to adapt and survive, but the continuity of archaic preconceptions, whose main role is to perpetuate the ancient Institution of Leadership and the System of Profound Privilege, works against improving existence and that which is needed for survival. Yet permanent change suggests the need for continuous examination of our metaphysical foundations – our individual and collective formatting that in any context affects human existence.

Upon reading this book, what actions will you take? How will you change? And what will you teach to others? As a leader, you have work to do that falls deeply within your scope of duties. Conflict is perhaps the most efficient way to waste resources, and it is ever-present in organizations due to the varied metaphysical foundations that exist within people or departments, as well as the overarching metaphysical foundations of business, economics, etc. The alternative is constant instability, complexity, chaos, and confusion. The dead hand of the past will always be our guide, but it should be to lesser extents rather than to greater extents.

There is a lot to worry about – too much to worry about – yet leaders must make the effort to imagine a better world and develop new skills and capabilities to move deliberatively in that direction. While pragmatism is revered, it too is rooted in preconceptions that limit leader's thinking and progress. Aphorisms, such as "better the devil you know" and "don't let perfect be the enemy of good" reflect that.

This book succinctly answers the question – "What do I have to do to become a better leader?" – at its root. As emerging leaders, you have some big challenges:

- Scrutinize your metaphysical foundation
- Examine what the leaders you most admire taught you, both implicitly and explicitly, or any authority figure
- Lead better than those who came before you
- Be aware of and find creative ways to manage the inevitable disputes and relationship problems that will arise

Progress means not just ideas about making things better such as reducing human suffering, improving the lives and livelihoods of workers, or assuring Earth's habitability, but implementation. To continue along with Chapter 1 preconceptions is to be neglectful of progress, if not a saboteur of progress. It means continuing the simplistic preconception that people should be blamed for problems – which means KRU-I, to not really solve problems and suffer ever-greater instability, versus the optimism and abilities that comes with KRU-II.

Leaders often talk of "excellence" and the need for it, and specifically the need for people at lower levels to deliver "excellence." Yet it should be clear that under KRU-I, "excellence" is a combination of empty rhetoric and unrealistic expectations placed onto others. The Foundational Preconceptions either disable the realization of "excellence" or limit it to what little is achievable under KRU-1 – a constellation of preconceptions devoid of trust [5]. To make progress towards "excellence," leaders must shift to KRU-II and develop the trust between leaders and followers that is missing from KRU-I. And there is much more practical opportunity in KRU-II than just that. A lifetime of discovery awaits emerging leaders.

This book can provide utility beyond the important but narrow frame of better leadership and management of organizations. Its utility spans from new product development to sales and marketing to organizational design to operations, and to corporate and business strategy. It can be used for getting individuals and groups of people to develop accurate understandings of difficult problems – from the shop floor or office to the boardroom in for-profit enterprises, non-profit enterprises, NGOs, and government – and then moving in the same direction towards progressive, rather than regressive (irrational), resolution. Much time and effort will be saved by unearthing the preconceptions that delay problem recognition and which lead to poor problem-solving.

I hope you enjoyed this book and that it has given you much to think about, and even more to do!

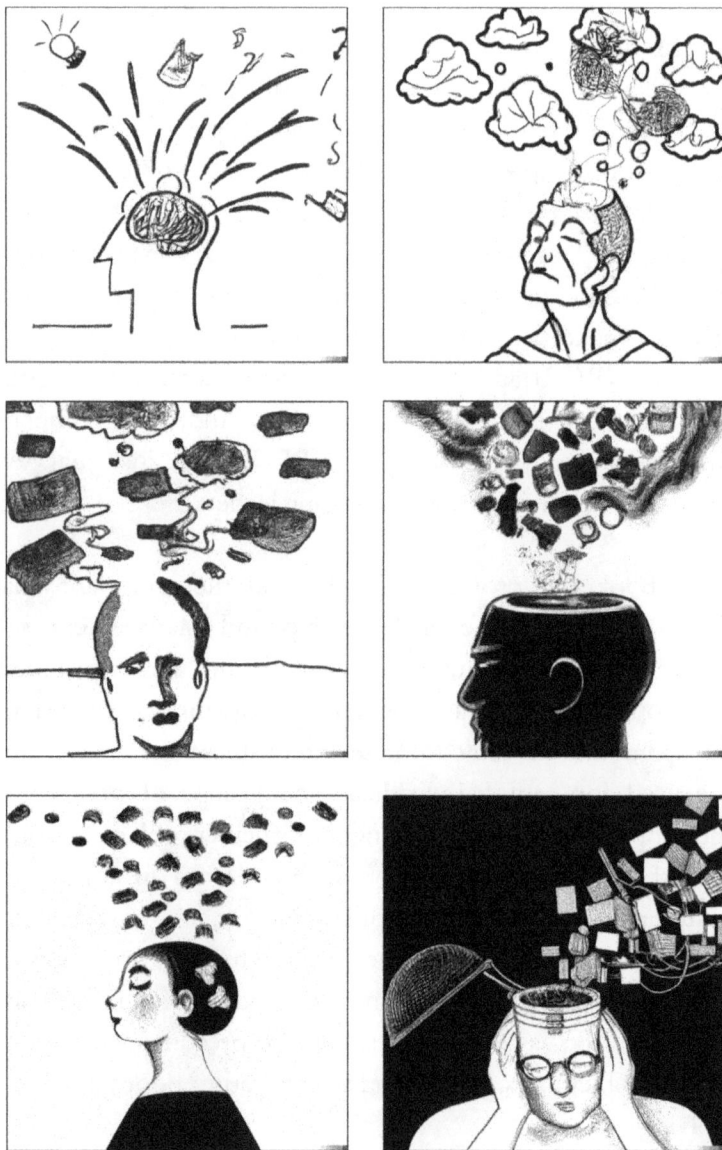

Figure 4-1. AI generated (DALL·E 2) images depicting the letting go of preconceptions that are archaic or no longer fit the times.

THINK

- What actions will you take?

THINK

- How will you change?

THINK

- What will you teach to others?

Notes

[1] It also suggests that beliefs are the same among all persons, as evidenced by the popular competency model construct, Behaviors → Competencies.

[2] I expect this will likely be ignored because the "change leader's behaviors" *zeitgeist* is so firmly rooted and because many people remain heavily invested in this tired and flawed idea. It remains a huge money-maker for trainers and consultants and disturbs the knowledge domains of the professional educators who teach it.

[3] In addition, one must also examine the contributions of cognitive biases and illogical thinking in failures, many or all of which may trace back to preconceptions. See Chapter 1, Note 10.

[4] Mitchell, W.C., (1970), *Types of Economic Theory: From Mercantilism to Institutionalism*, Volume 2, Joseph Dorfman, Ed., Augustus M. Kelley Publishers, New York, New York, p. 690

[5] A trust that is regularly, if not systematically, betrayed. When "excellence" is achieved, layoffs often follow. Additionally, technology (machines) play an important role in betrayal of trust, such as when leaders view workers as secondary or inferior to machines. This an important technological preconception.

About the Author

M.L. "Bob" Emiliani was a professor in the School of Engineering, Science, and Technology at Connecticut State University in New Britain, Conn., where he taught a graduate course on leadership, a unique course that analyzes failures in management decision-making, as well as other courses. He holds the honorary title of Professor Emeritus.

Bob earned a Bachelor of Science degree in mechanical engineering from the University of Miami, a Master of Science degree in chemical engineering from the University of Rhode Island, and a Doctor of Philosophy degree in engineering from Brown University.

He worked in the consumer products and aerospace industries for 15 years, beginning as a materials engineer. He has held management positions in engineering, manufacturing, and supply chain management at Pratt & Whitney. Bob joined academia in September 1999. While in academia, he developed a new teaching pedagogy and led activities to continuously improve master's degree programs.

Bob's curiosity led him to author or co-author 26 books, four book chapters, and more than 40 peer-reviewed papers in six different subject areas: leadership, management, management history, supply chain management, higher education, and materials engineering.

Please visit www.bobemiliani.com

Question Posed by Bob Emiliani
Which preconceptions are most effective at holding back progress?

Answer from OpenAIs ChatGPT Chatbot
There are many preconceptions that can hold back progress, but some common ones include:

Certain problems are unsolvable: This can lead to a lack of effort or resources being put towards finding solutions.

Certain approaches or technologies are superior to others: This can lead to a narrow-minded focus on a single approach or technology, even when it may not be the most effective solution.

Certain groups or individuals are incapable of achieving certain goals: This can lead to discrimination and inequality, and prevent people from reaching their full potential.

Change is always bad: This can lead to resistance to new ideas and a reluctance to embrace progress.

Status quo is always best: This can lead to a lack of innovation and a failure to adapt to changing circumstances.

It is important to be open-minded and to constantly question and evaluate our preconceptions in order to make progress and achieve our goals.

_____

Source: https://chat.openai.com/, ChatGPT Dec 15 Version, accessed 22 December 2022

Comment

The inherent weakness of any new concept, system, framework, process, method, tool, model, or practice whose intent it is to improve leadership and leadership decision-making (e.g., Scientific Management, Myers-Briggs Type Indicator, Emotional Intelligence, TQM, Lean management, Cynefin, etc.) – no matter how good and right it may be – is that it requires leaders to bow to reality in their everyday work, not just in times of crisis. It also requires leaders to routinely listen to people at the bottom of the social hierarchy, not just on special occasions – and do much more than take what they hear "into consideration." It requires them to relinquish the ancient mythologies of leadership as best they can. These are very difficult things for leaders to do owing to the magical origins of leadership and the need to preserve illusions. Additionally, and more importantly, these infringe upon leaders' rights, privileges, authority, freedom, entitlements, advantages, opportunities, benefits, and immunities from liability. It is a significant impediment past, present, and for the calculable future, not only for progress but for survival. It raises the critical question of what knowledge should be transferred from one generation to the next (i.e., that which sustains or refutes progress), and what advice should be given to younger generations (e.g., "Don't be bound to the past; think for yourself"). What knowledge is helpful, what knowledge is, or likely to be, harmful and should not be passed along? Information processing is the workmanship of leaders, and, as history reveals, it needs to be improved (see Chapter 1, Notes 9 and 10).

I am truly honored when people take time
from their precious life to read my work.

Thank you.